Pulpit O .... Series

www.pulpitoutlines.com

52 Sermons From the Gospel of John

By Barry L. Davis, D.Min.

Copyright©2013 Barry L. Davis

All Scripture taken from the King James Version.

PERMISSIONS: *If you are the purchaser of this volume you are given the right to use the following sermon outlines to preach/teach. You may use them "as is," or edit them to suit your purposes. You may not reproduce these outlines to give them away or offer them for sale. They are for the purchasers use only.*

Dear Fellow Preacher,

For most of us, one of the most rewarding, yet difficult tasks, is preparing messages to preach and teach. We are honored by God to stand before our congregation each week, and we want to give them the very best, but with the press of the many demands of ministry, sometimes that is difficult to do.

And if you're like me, you prefer writing your own sermons because you have a special connection with your congregation that is hard to reach through a message someone else has written. In other words, no one knows your people like you do!

Our new Pulpit Outline Series gives you a starting point – a sermon title, a deductive sermon outline; and a relevant illustration you can use however you like.

But you are free to "fill-in-the-blanks" so to speak, and add your own meat and potatoes to the mix! We invite you to make these messages your own, because only you know the people God has called you to preach to.

And we are so honored that you've invested in our second volume in the Pulpit Outline series – *52 Sermons from the Gospel of John* – there will be more to come!

May God Bless You as You Share His Word!

In Christ,
Barry L. Davis

www.pastorshelper.com I www.pulpitoutlines.com

Table of Contents

1. CHRIST, THE LIFE AND LIGHT OF MEN

John 1:1-5

ILLUSTRATION:

[1]The little village of Rattenberg is the smallest town in Austria, and getting smaller each year. The town has lost 20 percent of its population in the past two decades, and as of 2005 had only 440 residents. The reason? Darkness. Rattenberg is nestled behind Rat Mountain—a 3,000-foot obstruction that blocks out the sun from November to February. But thanks to some clever new technology, the town's situation is about to get a little brighter.

An Austrian company called Bartenbach Lichtlabor has come up with a plan to bring sunshine into the darkness by installing 30 heliostat mirrors onto the mountainside. The mirrors will grab light from reflectors on the sunny-side of the mountain and shine it back into the town.

The project will not be cheap—the European Union will cover half of the $2.4 million bill—but if successful, will bring hope to the 60 other communities scattered throughout the Alps that endure the winter darkness each year. Markus Peskoller, Lichtlabor's director, has also committed to paying for the $600,000 cost of planning the project because of its potential for other markets. "I am sure we will soon help other mountain villages see the light," he said.

John starts his Gospel with the time when God sent his own light into our world, through Jesus, and offered relief

---

[1] GEORGE JAHN, "MIRRORS TO BANISH TOWN'S WINTER DARKNESS," *Associated Press* (11-20-05)

from the darkness of our sin. And Christians all over the world who have experienced that forgiveness are called to reflect his light to those who still need it.

1. JESUS' RELATIONSHIP TO GOD THE FATHER

In the beginning was the Word, and the Word was with God, and the Word was God. The same was in the beginning with God. – John 1:1-2

That which was from the beginning, which we have heard, which we have seen with our eyes, which we have looked upon, and our hands have handled, of the Word of life; (For the life was manifested, and we have seen it, and bear witness, and shew unto you that eternal life, which was with the Father, and was manifested unto us;) – 1 John 1:1-2

2. JESUS' RELATIONSHIP TO CREATION

All things were made by him; and without him was not any thing made that was made. – John 1:3

And to make all men see what is the fellowship of the mystery, which from the beginning of the world hath been hid in God, who created all things by Jesus Christ. – Ephesians 3:9

Hath in these last days spoken unto us by his Son, whom he hath appointed heir of all things, by whom also he made the worlds. – Hebrews 1:2

Thou art worthy, O Lord, to receive glory and honour and power: for thou hast created all things, and for thy pleasure they are and were created. – Revelation 4:11

3. JESUS' RELATIONSHIP TO HUMANKIND

In him was life; and the life was the light of men. – John 1:4

And this is the record, that God hath given to us eternal life, and this life is in his Son. – 1 John 5:11

2. WHO MADE US SONS OF GOD?

John 1:6-13

ILLUSTRATION:

[2]"You sum up the whole of New Testament teaching in a single phrase, if you speak of it as a revelation of the Fatherhood of the holy Creator. In the same way, you sum up the whole of New Testament religion if you describe it as the knowledge of God as one's holy Father.

"If you want to judge how well a person understands Christianity, find out how much he makes of the thought of being God's child, and having God as his Father. If this is not the thought that prompts and controls his worship and prayers and his whole outlook on life, it means that he does not understand Christianity very well at all."

There was a man sent from God, whose name was John. The same came for a witness, to bear witness of the Light, that all men through him might believe. He was not that Light, but was sent to bear witness of that Light. That was the true Light, which lighteth every man that cometh into the world. – John 1:6-9

But as many as received him, to them gave he power to become the sons of God, even to them that believe on his name. – John 1:12

1. THE ONE WHO WAS IN THE WORLD

He was in the world, and the world was made by him, and the world knew him not. – John 1:10

---

[2] J. I. PACKER, KNOWING GOD, P. 182

2. THE ONE WHO MADE THE WORLD

He was in the world, and <u>the world was made by him</u>, and the world knew him not. – John 1:10

3. THE ONE WHO IS THE TRUE LIGHT

That was the true Light, which lighteth every man that cometh into the world. – John 1:9

4. THE ONE WHO WAS REJECTED BY HIS OWN

He was in the world, and the world was made by him, and <u>the world knew him not</u>. He came unto his own, and <u>his own received him not</u>. – John 1:10-11

5. THE ONE WHO HAS AUTHORITY TO MAKE US CHILDREN OF GOD

But as many as received him, to them gave he power to become the sons of God, even to them that believe on his name. – John 1:12

For ye have not received the spirit of bondage again to fear; but ye have received the Spirit of adoption, whereby we cry, Abba, Father. – Romans 8:15

For ye are all the children of God by faith in Christ Jesus. – Galatians 3:26

But when the fulness of the time was come, God sent forth his Son, made of a woman, made under the law, To redeem them that were under the law, that we might receive the adoption of sons. – Galatians 4:4-5

6. THE ONE WHO HAS POWER TO REGENERATE THE SOUL

Which were born, not of blood, nor of the will of the flesh, nor of the will of man, but of God. – John 1:13

3. THE WORD MADE FLESH

John 1:14-18

ILLUSTRATION:

[3]In September of 2006, Sociologists from Baylor University released the results of a study looking into America's different views of God. Part of the study was a survey conducted by the Gallup organization, which identified four distinct views of God's personality and interaction with the world. Baylor researchers outlined the results as follows:

Thos who believe in an "Authoritarian God" who is "angry at humanity's sins and engaged in every creature's life and world affairs": 31.4 percent.

Those who believe in a "Benevolent God" who is forgiving and accepting of anyone who repents: 23 percent.

Those who believe in a "Critical God" who "has his judgmental eye on the world, but he's not going to intervene, either to punish or comfort": 16 percent.

Those who believe in a "Distant God" who is more of a "cosmic force that launched the world, then left it spinning on its own": 24.4 percent.

Today we will look at the Biblical view of God, as demonstrated in the coming of Jesus to this earth.

1. A MYSTERIOUS INCARNATION

---

[3] CATHY LUNN-GROSSMAN, "AMERICAN'S IMAGE OF GOD VARIES," *USAToday.com* (9-11-06)

And <u>the Word was made flesh</u>, and dwelt among us, (and we beheld his glory, the glory as of the only begotten of the Father,) full of grace and truth. – John 1:14

2. A PROFOUND HUMILIATION

And the Word was made flesh, <u>and dwelt among us</u>, (and we beheld his glory, the glory as of the only begotten of the Father,) full of grace and truth. – John 1:14

3. A DIVINE MANIFESTATION

No man hath seen God at any time; the only begotten Son, which is in the bosom of the Father, he hath declared him. – John 1:18

All things are delivered unto me of my Father: and no man knoweth the Son, but the Father; neither knoweth any man the Father, save the Son, and he to whomsoever the Son will reveal him. – Matthew 11:27

I have manifested thy name unto the men which thou gavest me out of the world: thine they were, and thou gavest them me; and they have kept thy word. – John 17:6

4. A PROVIDED SALVATION

And the Word was made flesh, and dwelt among us, (and we beheld his glory, the glory as of the only begotten of the Father,) <u>full of grace and truth</u>. – John 1:14

For the law was given by Moses, but grace and truth came by Jesus Christ. – John 1:17

Mercy and truth are met together; righteousness and peace have kissed each other. – Psalms 85:10

For if the ministration of condemnation be glory, much more doth the ministration of righteousness exceed in glory. – 2 Corinthians 3:9

5. A BLESSED TESTIMONY

And the Word was made flesh, and dwelt among us, (and <u>we beheld his glory</u>, the glory as of the only begotten of the Father,) full of grace and truth. John bare witness of him, and cried, saying, This was he of whom I spake, He that cometh after me is preferred before me: for he was before me. <u>And of his fulness have all we received</u>, and grace for grace. – John 1:14-16

4. WHAT JOHN SAID ABOUT JESUS

John 1:29-34

ILLUSTRATION:

[4]Joshua Bell emerged from the Metro and positioned himself against a wall beside a trash basket. By most measures, he was nondescript—a youngish white man in jeans, a long-sleeved T-shirt, and a Washington Nationals baseball cap. From a small case, he removed a violin. Placing the open case at his feet, he shrewdly threw in a few dollars and pocket change as seed money and began to play.

For the next 45 minutes, in the D.C. Metro on January 12, 2007, Bell played Mozart and Schubert as over 1,000 people streamed by, most hardly taking notice. If they had paid attention, they might have recognized the young man for the world-renowned violinist he is. They also might have noted the violin he played—a rare Stradivarius worth over $3 million. It was all part of a project arranged by THE WASHINGTON POST—"an experiment in context, perception, and priorities—as well as an unblinking assessment of public taste. In a banal setting, at an inconvenient time, would beauty transcend?"

Just three days earlier, Joshua Bell sold out Boston Symphony Hall, with ordinary seats going for $100. In the subway, Bell garnered about $32 from the 27 people who stopped long enough to give a donation.

1. JESUS IS THE LAMB OF GOD

---

[4] GENE WEINGARTEN, "PEARLS BEFORE BREAKFAST," *The Washington Post* (4-10-07)

The next day John seeth Jesus coming unto him, and saith, Behold the Lamb of God, which taketh away the sin of the world. – John 1:29

And he is the propitiation for our sins: and not for ours only, but also for the sins of the whole world. – 1 John 2:2

And all that dwell upon the earth shall worship him, whose names are not written in the book of life of the Lamb slain from the foundation of the world. – Revelation 13:8

Herein is love, not that we loved God, but that he loved us, and sent his Son to be the propitiation for our sins. – 1 John 4:10

2. JESUS WAS BEFORE ME

This is he of whom I said, After me cometh a man which is preferred before me: for he was before me. – John 1:30

The same was in the beginning with God. – John 1:2

3. JESUS WOULD BE MADE MANIFEST TO ISRAEL

And I knew him not: but that he should be made manifest to Israel, therefore am I come baptizing with water. – John 1:31

4. JESUS IS THE ANOINTED ONE

And John bare record, saying, I saw the Spirit descending from heaven like a dove, and it abode upon him. – John 1:32

But ye shall receive power, after that the Holy Ghost is come upon you: and ye shall be witnesses unto me both in Jerusalem, and in all Judaea, and in Samaria, and unto the uttermost part of the earth. – Acts 1:8

5. JESUS IS THE ONE WHO BAPTIZES WITH THE HOLY SPIRIT

And I knew him not: but he that sent me to baptize with water, the same said unto me, Upon whom thou shalt see the Spirit descending, and remaining on him, the same is he which baptizeth with the Holy Ghost. – John 1:33

6. JESUS IS THE SON OF GOD

And I saw, and bare record that this is the Son of God. Again the next day after John stood, and two of his disciples; And looking upon Jesus as he walked, he saith, Behold the Lamb of God! – John 1:34-36

I said therefore unto you, that ye shall die in your sins: for if ye believe not that I am he, ye shall die in your sins. – John 8:24

5. THE FIRST DISCIPLES

John 1:35-42

ILLUSTRATION:

[5]Rich Stearns, the president of World Vision, calls it the domino theory of spiritual impact. Imagine a long line of dominoes. When one falls, it starts a chain reaction that can cause dozens or hundreds more dominoes to fall. For instance, Jesus set up 12 dominoes (his disciples), mentored them, empowered them with the Holy Spirit, and then sent them off to go and do likewise. Now there are over 2 billion followers of Christ in the world. That's a lot of dominoes!

Stearns provides the following story about the spiritual impact that one person can have. In the 1880s, Robert Wilder, a missionary kid from India, was preparing to return to the mission field. During college, he even signed a pledge along with friends to become a missionary. But because he was so physically frail, he never fulfilled that pledge. Instead, he encouraged others to take up the task. ONE DOMINO FELL.

During a preaching tour that took Robert through Chicago, he spoke to an audience that included Samuel Moffett. Samuel also signed Robert's pledge, and within two years he landed in Korea. ANOTHER DOMINO FELL.

A few years later, Samuel shared the gospel with a man who had become disillusioned with his Taoist practice.

---

[5] RICH STEARNS, "SPIRITUAL DOMINOES," *World Vision Magazine* (WINTER 2011)

Kiel Sun-chu trusted Christ, and quickly ANOTHER DOMINO FELL.

In 1907, Kiel was one of the leaders of the Pyongyang revival. In January of that year, spontaneous prayer and confession broke out during regular church meetings. THOUSANDS OF DOMINOES FELL. Those days of fervent prayer are now considered the birth of an independent, self-sustaining Korean church.

When Kiel died in 1935, 5,000 people attended his funeral. The church in Korea now numbers about 15 million, and it sends more foreign missionaries than any other country outside the United States. MILLIONS OF DOMINOES CONTINUE TO FALL.

Stearns concludes:

As Christians, we are all dominoes in the chain reaction set off by Jesus 2,000 years ago. The amazing thing about dominoes falling is that the chain reaction always starts small—with just one, seemingly insignificant domino. Whether you are sponsoring children, filling backpacks for children in inner-city schools, talking to your own children, or praying earnestly for [people around the globe], you have no idea what how big the impact will be as God multiplies your faithfulness.

1. A SIMPLE TESTIMONY

Again the next day after John stood, and two of his disciples; And looking upon Jesus as he walked, he saith, Behold the Lamb of God! – John 1:35-36

2. AN ACT OF FAITH

And the two disciples heard him speak, and they followed Jesus. – John 1:37

3. A HEART-SEARCHING QUESTION

Then Jesus turned, and saw them following, and saith unto them, <u>What seek ye</u>? They said unto him, Rabbi, (which is to say, being interpreted, Master,) where dwellest thou? – John 1:38

Then said Jesus unto his disciples, If any man will come after me, let him deny himself, and take up his cross, and follow me. – Matthew 16:24

4. AN ANXIOUS INQUIRY

Then Jesus turned, and saw them following, and saith unto them, What seek ye? They said unto him, Rabbi, (which is to say, being interpreted, Master,) <u>where dwellest thou</u>? – John 1:38

No man hath seen God at any time; the only begotten Son, <u>which is in the bosom of the Father</u>, he hath declared him. – John 1:18

5. A GRACIOUS INVITATION

He saith unto them, Come and see. They came and saw where he dwelt, and abode with him that day: for it was about the tenth hour. – John 1:39

Come unto me, all ye that labour and are heavy laden, and I will give you rest. – Matthew 11:28

6. A WILLING SERVICE

One of the two which heard John speak, and followed him, was Andrew, Simon Peter's brother. He first findeth his own brother Simon, and saith unto him, We have found the Messias, which is, being interpreted, the Christ. And he brought him to Jesus. And when Jesus beheld him, he said, Thou art Simon the son of Jona: thou shalt be called Cephas, which is by interpretation, A stone. – John 1:40-42

Herein is my Father glorified, that ye bear much fruit; so shall ye be my disciples. – John 15:8

6. NATHANAEL'S CONVERSION

John 1:43-51

ILLUSTRATION:

[6]If you were doomed to live the same life over and over again for eternity, would you choose the life you are living now? The question is interesting enough, but I've always thought the point of asking it is really the unspoken, potentially devastating follow-up question. That is, if the answer is no, then why ARE you living the life you are living now? Stop making excuses, and do something about it.

1. HE HEARD

Philip findeth Nathanael, and saith unto him, We have found him, of whom Moses in the law, and the prophets, did write, Jesus of Nazareth, the son of Joseph. – John 1:45

2. HE QUESTIONED

And Nathanael said unto him, Can there any good thing come out of Nazareth? Philip saith unto him, Come and see. – John 1:46

And he came and dwelt in a city called Nazareth: that it might be fulfilled which was spoken by the prophets, He shall be called a Nazarene. – Matthew 2:23

3. HE PROVED

---

[6] WILLIAM ALEXANDER, *The $64 Tomato* (ALGONQUIN BOOKS, 2007), P. 245

Jesus saw Nathanael coming to him, and saith of him, Behold an Israelite indeed, in whom is no guile! Nathanael saith unto him, Whence knowest thou me? Jesus answered and said unto him, Before that Philip called thee, when thou wast under the fig tree, I saw thee. – John 1:47-48

4. HE CONFESSED

Nathanael answered and saith unto him, Rabbi, thou art the Son of God; thou art the King of Israel. – John 1:49

Nevertheless among the chief rulers also many believed on him; but because of the Pharisees they did not confess him, lest they should be put out of the synagogue: For they loved the praise of men more than the praise of God. – John 12:42-43

Whosoever therefore shall confess me before men, him will I confess also before my Father which is in heaven. – Matthew 10:32

5. HE BELIEVED

Jesus answered and said unto him, Because I said unto thee, I saw thee under the fig tree, believest thou? thou shalt see greater things than these. – John 1:50

6. HE WAS ENCOURAGED

And he saith unto him, Verily, verily, I say unto you, Hereafter ye shall see heaven open, and the angels of God ascending and descending upon the Son of man. – John 1:51

7. THE FIRST SIGN

John 2:1-11

ILLUSTRATION:

[7]One Communion Sunday in our Massachusetts church, the deacon in charge inadvertently substituted cranberry juice for grape juice. In true New England fashion, some of the congregation, upon the passing of this "new wine" over their tongues, wanted desperately to gag, but couldn't because of the solemnity of the moment. As I gazed at the puckered-up faces, I had to refrain from shouting, "He did it again! He did it again!"

This beginning of miracles did Jesus in Cana of Galilee, and manifested forth his glory; and his disciples believed on him. – John 2:11

1. THE OCCASION

And the third day there was a marriage in Cana of Galilee; and the mother of Jesus was there: And both Jesus was called, and his disciples, to the marriage. And when they wanted wine, the mother of Jesus saith unto him, They have no wine. – John 2:1-3

2. THE MEANING

It was the manifestation of the-

1. **Glory of His All-sufficient Grace**.

---

[7] REV. J. CLIFFORD DAVID, MILLBURY, MASS. "LITE FARE," CHRISTIAN READER.

And the Word was made flesh, and dwelt among us, (and we beheld his glory, the glory as of the only begotten of the Father,) full of grace and truth. – John 1:14

2. **Glory of His Transforming Power**.

I beseech you therefore, brethren, by the mercies of God, that ye present your bodies a living sacrifice, holy, acceptable unto God, which is your reasonable service. And be not conformed to this world: but be ye transformed by the renewing of your mind, that ye may prove what is that good, and acceptable, and perfect, will of God. – Romans 12:1-2

3. **Glory of His Unmatched Character**.

And saith unto him, Every man at the beginning doth set forth good wine; and when men have well drunk, then that which is worse: but thou hast kept the good wine until now. – John 2:10

Let us be glad and rejoice, and give honour to him: for the marriage of the Lamb is come, and his wife hath made herself ready. – Revelation 19:7

8. CLEANSING THE TEMPLE

John 2:13-19

ILLUSTRATION:

[8]David McCullough in his book MORNINGS ON HORSEBACK tells this story about young Teddy Roosevelt:

"Mittie (his mother) had found he was so afraid of the Madison Square Church that he refused to set foot inside if alone. He was terrified, she discovered, of something called the 'zeal.' It was crouched in the dark corners of the church ready to jump at him, he said. When she asked what a zeal might be, he said he was not sure, but thought it was probably a large animal like an alligator or a dragon. He had heard the minister read about it from the Bible. Using a concordance, she read him those passages containing the word 'zeal' until suddenly, very excited, he told her to stop. The line was from the Book of John, (John 2)17: "And his disciples remembered that it was written, 'The zeal of thine house hath eaten me up.' "

People are still justifiably afraid to come near the "zeal" of the Lord, for they are perfectly aware it could "eat them up" if they aren't one of his. Our Lord is good, but he isn't safe.

1. THE TEMPLE DEFILED

And found in the temple those that sold oxen and sheep and doves, and the changers of money sitting. – John 2:14

---

[8] GREG WEBB, LEADERSHIP, VOL. 10, NO. 1.

And what agreement hath the temple of God with idols? for ye are the temple of the living God; as God hath said, I will dwell in them, and walk in them; and I will be their God, and they shall be my people. – 2 Corinthians 6:16

2. THE TEMPLE CLEANSED

And when he had made a scourge of small cords, he drove them all out of the temple, and the sheep, and the oxen; and poured out the changers' money, and overthrew the tables; And said unto them that sold doves, Take these things hence; make not my Father's house an house of merchandise. – John 2:15-16

Behold, I will send my messenger, and he shall prepare the way before me: and the Lord, whom ye seek, shall suddenly come to his temple, even the messenger of the covenant, whom ye delight in: behold, he shall come, saith the LORD of hosts. But who may abide the day of his coming? and who shall stand when he appeareth? for he is like a refiner's fire, and like fullers' soap: And he shall sit as a refiner and purifier of silver: and he shall purify the sons of Levi, and purge them as gold and silver, that they may offer unto the LORD an offering in righteousness. – Malachi 3:1-3

3. THE TEMPLE CLEANSER

And his disciples remembered that it was written, The zeal of thine house hath eaten me up. Then answered the Jews and said unto him, What sign shewest thou unto us, seeing that thou doest these things? Jesus answered and said unto them, Destroy this temple, and in three days I will raise it up. Then said the Jews, Forty and six years was this temple in building, and wilt thou rear it up in three days? But he spake of the temple of his body. When therefore he was risen from the dead, his disciples remembered that he had said this unto them; and they believed the scripture, and the word which Jesus had said. – John 2:17-22

But he answered and said unto them, An evil and adulterous generation seeketh after a sign; and there shall no sign be given to it, but the sign of the prophet Jonas: For as Jonas was three days and three nights in the whale's belly; so shall the Son of man be three days and three nights in the heart of the earth. – Matthew 12:39-40

9. THE NEW BIRTH

John 3:1-9

ILLUSTRATION:

[9]Every animal on earth has a set of correspondences with the environment around it, and some of those correspondences far exceed ours. Humans can perceive only thirty percent of the range of the sun's light and 1/70th of the spectrum of electromagnetic energy. Many animals exceed our abilities. Bats detect insects by sonar; pigeons navigate by magnetic fields; bloodhounds perceive a world of smell unavailable to us.

Perhaps the spiritual or "unseen" world requires an inbuilt set of correspondences activated only through some sort of spiritual quickening. "No one can see the kingdom of God without being born from above," said Jesus. "The man without the Spirit does not accept the things that come from the Spirit of God, for they are foolishness to him, and he cannot understand them, because they are spiritually discerned," said Paul. Both expressions point to a different level of correspondence available only to a person spiritually alive.

1. IT IS A NECESSITY TO THE KINGDOM OF GOD

There was a man of the Pharisees, named Nicodemus, a ruler of the Jews: The same came to Jesus by night, and said unto him, Rabbi, we know that thou art a teacher come from God: for no man can do these miracles that thou doest, except God be with him. Jesus answered and

---

[9] PHILIP YANCEY, "SEEING THE INVISIBLE GOD" BOOKS AND CULTURE (MAY/JUNE 2000), P.8

said unto him, Verily, verily, I say unto thee, Except a man be born again, he cannot see the kingdom of God. Nicodemus saith unto him, How can a man be born when he is old? can he enter the second time into his mother's womb, and be born? Jesus answered, Verily, verily, I say unto thee, Except a man be born of water and of the Spirit, he cannot enter into the kingdom of God. – John 3:1-5

Which were born, not of blood, nor of the will of the flesh, nor of the will of man, but of God. – John 1:13

Therefore if any man be in Christ, he is a new creature: old things are passed away; behold, all things are become new. – 2 Corinthians 5:17

2. IT IS A MYSTERY TO THE NATURAL MAN

Nicodemus saith unto him, How can a man be born when he is old? can he enter the second time into his mother's womb, and be born? – John 3:4

But the natural man receiveth not the things of the Spirit of God: for they are foolishness unto him: neither can he know them, because they are spiritually discerned. – 1 Corinthians 2:14

And the light shineth in darkness; and the darkness comprehended it not. – John 1:5

3. IT IS THE WORK OF THE HOLY SPIRIT

That which is born of the flesh is flesh; and that which is born of the Spirit is spirit. Marvel not that I said unto thee, Ye must be born again. The wind bloweth where it listeth, and thou hearest the sound thereof, but canst not tell whence it cometh, and whither it goeth: so is every one that is born of the Spirit. – John 3:6-8

It is the spirit that quickeneth; the flesh profiteth nothing: the words that I speak unto you, they are spirit, and they are life. – John 6:63

For to be carnally minded is death; but to be spiritually minded is life and peace. Because the carnal mind is enmity against God: for it is not subject to the law of God, neither indeed can be. So then they that are in the flesh cannot please God. But ye are not in the flesh, but in the Spirit, if so be that the Spirit of God dwell in you. Now if any man have not the Spirit of Christ, he is none of his. – Romans 8:6-9

10. THE WAY INTO LIFE

John 3:14-21

ILLUSTRATION:

[10]Fort Hancock is on the farthest tip of Sandy Hook, which reaches out into the Atlantic on the New Jersey coast. During World War II it was a military training center. A civilian of the area was eager to bring the good news of Christ to the thousands of young men stationed there. The military authorities would not permit him to enter in person. Not to be denied, he asked a firm that specialized in novelties to make several thousand mirrors about three inches in diameter. On the back of each mirror he had printed the words of John 3:16. Beneath these words he had this direction, "If you want to see who it is that God loves, look on the other side." As each soldier looked at himself he saw the person whom God loved.

1. A GREAT NEED

And as Moses lifted up the serpent in the wilderness, even so must the Son of man be lifted up: That whosoever believeth in him should not perish, but have eternal life. – John 3:14-15

Neither is there salvation in any other: for there is none other name under heaven given among men, whereby we must be saved. – Acts 4:12

2. A GREAT LOVE

---

[10] Source unknown.

For God so loved the world, that he gave his only begotten Son, that whosoever believeth in him should not perish, but have everlasting life. – John 3:16

But God commendeth his love toward us, in that, while we were yet sinners, Christ died for us. – Romans 5:8

He that spared not his own Son, but delivered him up for us all, how shall he not with him also freely give us all things? – Romans 8:32

3. A GREAT SUFFERING

Then said Jesus unto them, When ye have lifted up the Son of man, then shall ye know that I am he, and that I do nothing of myself; but as my Father hath taught me, I speak these things. – John 8:28

Take heed therefore unto yourselves, and to all the flock, over the which the Holy Ghost hath made you overseers, to feed the church of God, which he hath purchased with his own blood. – Acts 20:28

4. A GREAT PURPOSE

For God sent not his Son into the world to condemn the world; but that the world through him might be saved. – John 3:17

In that day there shall be a fountain opened to the house of David and to the inhabitants of Jerusalem for sin and for uncleanness. – Zechariah 13:1

5. A GREAT PRIVILEGE

That whosoever believeth in him should not perish, but have eternal life. For God so loved the world, that he gave his only begotten Son, that whosoever believeth in him should not perish, but have everlasting life. – John 3:15-16

He that believeth on him is not condemned: but he that believeth not is condemned already, because he hath not believed in the name of the only begotten Son of God. – John 3:18

6. A GREAT RESPONSIBILITY

And this is the condemnation, that light is come into the world, and men loved darkness rather than light, because their deeds were evil. For every one that doeth evil hateth the light, neither cometh to the light, lest his deeds should be reproved. But he that doeth truth cometh to the light, that his deeds may be made manifest, that they are wrought in God. – John 3:19-21

11. JOHN'S LAST TESTIMONY

John 3:25-36

ILLUSTRATION:

[11]Every young student knows of Isaac Newton's famed encounter with a falling apple. Newton discovered and introduced the laws of gravity in the 1600s, which revolutionized astronomical studies. But few know that if it weren't for Edmund Halley, the world might never have learned from Newton.

It was Halley who challenged Newton to think through his original notions. Halley corrected Newton's mathematical errors and prepared geometrical figures to support his discoveries. Halley coaxed the hesitant Newton to write his great work, MATHEMATICAL PRINCIPALS OF NATURAL PHILOSOPHY. Halley edited and supervised the publication, and actually financed its printing even though Newton was wealthier and easily could have afforded the printing costs. Historians call it one of the most selfless examples in the annals of science.

Newton began almost immediately to reap the rewards of prominence; Halley received little credit. He did use the principles to predict the orbit and return of the comet that would later bear his name, but only after his death did he received any acclaim. And because the comet only returns every seventy-six years, the notice is rather infrequent. Halley remained a devoted scientist who didn't care who received the credit as long as the cause was being advanced.

---

[11] C.S. KIRKENDALL, JR., KNOXVILLE, TENNESSEE. LEADERSHIP, VOL. 7, NO. 1.

Others have played Halley's role. John the Baptist said of Jesus, "He must become greater; I must become less." Barnabas was content to introduce others to greatness. Many pray to uphold the work of one Christian leader. Such selflessness advances the kingdom.

Then there arose a question between some of John's disciples and the Jews about purifying. And they came unto John, and said unto him, Rabbi, he that was with thee beyond Jordan, to whom thou barest witness, behold, the same baptizeth, and all men come to him. – John 3:25-26

1. ALL CHRISTIAN SUCCESS COMES FROM GOD

John answered and said, A man can receive nothing, except it be given him from heaven. – John 3:27

Every good gift and every perfect gift is from above, and cometh down from the Father of lights, with whom is no variableness, neither shadow of turning. – James 1:17

2. THE TRUE FRIENDS OF CHRIST REJOICE IN HIS EXALTATION

He that hath the bride is the bridegroom: but the friend of the bridegroom, which standeth and heareth him, rejoiceth greatly because of the bridegroom's voice: this my joy therefore is fulfilled. He must increase, but I must decrease. – John 3:29-30

Henceforth I call you not servants; for the servant knoweth not what his lord doeth: but I have called you friends; for all things that I have heard of my Father I have made known unto you. – John 15:15

3. HE THAT COMES FROM ABOVE IS ABOVE ALL

He that cometh from above is above all: he that is of the earth is earthly, and speaketh of the earth: he that cometh from heaven is above all. – John 3:31

For we wrestle not against flesh and blood, but against principalities, against powers, against the rulers of the darkness of this world, against spiritual wickedness in high places. Wherefore take unto you the whole armour of God, that ye may be able to withstand in the evil day, and having done all, to stand. – Ephesians 6:12-13

4. TO RECEIVE CHRIST'S TESTIMONY IS TO HONOR GOD

He that hath received his testimony hath set to his seal that God is true. For he whom God hath sent speaketh the words of God: for God giveth not the Spirit by measure unto him. – John 3:33-34

He that believeth on the Son of God hath the witness in himself: he that believeth not God hath made him a liar; because he believeth not the record that God gave of his Son. – 1 John 5:10

For even the Son of man came not to be ministered unto, but to minister, and to give his life a ransom for many. – Mark 10:45

5. THE FATHER HAS HONORED THE SON IN EVERYTHING

The Father loveth the Son, and hath given all things into his hand. – John 3:35

For the Father loveth the Son, and sheweth him all things that himself doeth: and he will shew him greater works than these, that ye may marvel. For as the Father raiseth up the dead, and quickeneth them; even so the Son quickeneth whom he will. For the Father judgeth no man, but hath committed all judgment unto the Son. – John 5:20-22

Jesus knowing that the Father had given all things into his hands, and that he was come from God, and went to God. – John 13:3

As thou hast given him power over all flesh, that he should give eternal life to as many as thou hast given him. – John 17:2

Thou hast put all things in subjection under his feet. For in that he put all in subjection under him, he left nothing that is not put under him. But now we see not yet all things put under him. – Hebrews 2:8

And Jesus came and spake unto them, saying, All power is given unto me in heaven and in earth. – Matthew 28:18

Of the increase of his government and peace there shall be no end, upon the throne of David, and upon his kingdom, to order it, and to establish it with judgment and with justice from henceforth even for ever. The zeal of the LORD of hosts will perform this. – Isaiah 9:7

For in him dwelleth all the fulness of the Godhead bodily. – Colossians 2:9

6. TO BELIEVE ON THE SON IS TO HAVE EVERLASTING LIFE

He that believeth on the Son hath everlasting life: and he that believeth not the Son shall not see life; but the wrath of God abideth on him. – John 3:36

As thou hast given him power over all flesh, that he should give eternal life to as many as thou hast given him. – John 17:2

I said therefore unto you, that ye shall die in your sins: for if ye believe not that I am he, ye shall die in your sins. – John 8:24

7. TO DISBELIEVE THE SON IS TO ABIDE UNDER THE WRATH OF GOD

He that believeth on the Son hath everlasting life: and he that believeth not the Son shall not see life; but the wrath of God abideth on him. – John 3:36

For the wrath of God is revealed from heaven against all ungodliness and unrighteousness of men, who hold the truth in unrighteousness. – Romans 1:18

For whoremongers, for them that defile themselves with mankind, for menstealers, for liars, for perjured persons, and if there be any other thing that is contrary to sound doctrine. – 1 Timothy 1:10

12. THE LIVING WATER

John 4:7-14

ILLUSTRATION:

[12]In the 19th century Charles Bradlaugh, a prominent atheist, challenged a Christian man to debate the validity of the claims of Christianity. The Christian was Hugh Price Hughes, an active soul-winner who worked among the poor in the slums of London. Hughes told Bradlaugh he would agree to the debate on one condition.

Hughes said, "I propose to you that we each bring some concrete evidences of the validity of our beliefs in the form of men and women who have been redeemed from the lives of sin and shame by the influence of our teaching. I will bring 100 such men and women, and I challenge you to do the same."

Hughes then said that if Bradlaugh couldn't bring 100, then he could bring 20. He finally whittled the number down to one. All Bradlaugh had to do was to find one person whose life was improved by atheism, and Hughes—who would bring 100 people improved by Christ—would agree to debate him. Bradlaugh withdrew!

There cometh a woman of Samaria to draw water: Jesus saith unto her, Give me to drink. (For his disciples were gone away unto the city to buy meat.) Then saith the woman of Samaria unto him, How is it that thou, being a Jew, askest drink of me, which am a woman of Samaria?

---

[12] D. JAMES KENNEDY AND JERRY NEWCOMBE, WHAT IF JESUS HAD NEVER BEEN BORN? (THOMAS NELSON, 1997), P. 189

for the Jews have no dealings with the Samaritans. – John 4:7-9

1. THE NATURE OF IT

Jesus answered and said unto her, If thou knewest the gift of God, and who it is that saith to thee, Give me to drink; thou wouldest have asked of him, and he would have given thee living water. – John 4:10

For by grace are ye saved through faith; and that not of yourselves: it is the gift of God. – Ephesians 2:8

2. THE SOURCE OF IT

As thou hast given him power over all flesh, that he should give eternal life to as many as thou hast given him. – John 17:2

And he shewed me a pure river of water of life, clear as crystal, proceeding out of the throne of God and of the Lamb. – Revelation 22:1

3. THE EFFECTIVENESS OF IT

1. **It Quenches Thirst**.

But whosoever drinketh of the water that I shall give him <u>shall never thirst</u>; but the water that I shall give him shall be in him a well of water springing up into everlasting life. – John 4:14

2. **It Becomes a Spring Within**.

But whosoever drinketh of the water that I shall give him shall never thirst; but the water that I shall give him shall be in him a well of water springing up into everlasting life. – John 4:14

4. THE CONDITIONS OF IT

Jesus answered and said unto her, If thou knewest the gift of God, and who it is that saith to thee, Give me to drink; thou wouldest have asked of him, and he would have given thee living water. – John 4:10

5. THE FREENESS OF IT

But whosoever drinketh of the water that I shall give him shall never thirst; but the water that I shall give him shall be in him a well of water springing up into everlasting life. – John 4:14

And the Spirit and the bride say, Come. And let him that heareth say, Come. And let him that is athirst come. And whosoever will, let him take the water of life freely. – Revelation 22:17

13. THE WOMAN OF SAMARIA

John 4:1-30

ILLUSTRATION:

[13]In his book SAHARA UNVEILED, William Langewiesche tells the story of an Algerian named Lag Lag and a companion whose truck broke down while crossing the desert:

They nearly died of thirst during the three weeks they waited before being rescued. As their bodies dehydrated, they became willing to drink anything in hopes of quenching their terrible thirst. The sun forced them into the shade under the truck, where they dug a shallow trench. Day after day they lay there. They had food, but did not eat, fearing it would magnify their thirst. Dehydration, not starvation, kills wanderers in the desert, and thirst is the most terrible of all human sufferings.

Physiologists use Greek-based words to describe stages of human thirst. For example, the Sahara is dipsogenic, meaning "thirst provoking."

In Lag Lag's case, they might say he progressed from eudipsia, "ordinary thirst," through bouts of hyperdipsia, meaning "temporary intense thirst," to polydipsia, "sustained excessive thirst." Polydipsia means the kind of thirst that drives one to drink anything. There are specialized terms for such behavior, including uriposia, the drinking of urine, and hemoposia, the drinking of blood.

---

[13] WILLIAM LANGEWIESCHE, SAHARA UNVEILED (VINTAGE, 1997)

For word enthusiasts, this is heady stuff. Nevertheless, the lexicon has not kept up with technology. I have tried, and cannot coin a suitable word for the drinking of rusty radiator water. Radiator water is what Lag Lag and his assistant started into when good drinking water was gone. In order to survive, they were willing to drink, in effect, poison.

Many people do something similar in the spiritual realm. They depend on things like money, sex, and power to quench spiritual thirst. Unfortunately, such "thirst quenchers" are in reality spiritual poison, a dangerous substitute for the "living water" Jesus promised.

1. A FLAGRANT SINNER

For thou hast had five husbands; and he whom thou now hast is not thy husband: in that saidst thou truly. – John 4:18

2. AN AWAKENED QUESTIONER

Then saith the woman of Samaria unto him, How is it that thou, being a Jew, askest drink of me, which am a woman of Samaria? for the Jews have no dealings with the Samaritans. – John 4:9

Then answered the Jews, and said unto him, Say we not well that thou art a Samaritan, and hast a devil? – John 8:48

3. A CARNAL REASONER

Jesus answered and said unto her, If thou knewest the gift of God, and who it is that saith to thee, Give me to drink; thou wouldest have asked of him, and he would have given thee living water. The woman saith unto him, Sir, thou hast nothing to draw with, and the well is deep: from whence then hast thou that living water? – John 4:10-11

But the natural man receiveth not the things of the Spirit of God: for they are foolishness unto him: neither can he know them, because they are spiritually discerned. – 1 Corinthians 2:14

4. A BEWILDERED WONDERER

The woman saith unto him, Sir, give me this water, that I thirst not, neither come hither to draw. – John 4:15

5. A RELIGIOUS INQUIRER

Jesus saith unto her, Go, call thy husband, and come hither. The woman answered and said, I have no husband. Jesus said unto her, Thou hast well said, I have no husband: For thou hast had five husbands; and he whom thou now hast is not thy husband: in that saidst thou truly. The woman saith unto him, Sir, I perceive that thou art a prophet. Our fathers worshipped in this mountain; and ye say, that in Jerusalem is the place where men ought to worship. – John 4:16-20

6. AN EARNEST LISTENER

Jesus saith unto her, Woman, believe me, the hour cometh, when ye shall neither in this mountain, nor yet at Jerusalem, worship the Father. Ye worship ye know not what: we know what we worship: for salvation is of the Jews. But the hour cometh, and now is, when the true worshippers shall worship the Father in spirit and in truth: for the Father seeketh such to worship him. God is a Spirit: and they that worship him must worship him in spirit and in truth. – John 4:21-24

7. A FEARLESS TESTIFIER

The woman then left her waterpot, and went her way into the city, and saith to the men, Come, see a man, which told me all things that ever I did: is not this the Christ? Then they went out of the city, and came unto him. – John 4:28-30

And many of the Samaritans of that city believed on him for the saying of the woman, which testified, He told me all that ever I did. – John 4:39

14. FAITH: ITS NATURE AND REWARD

John 4:46-54

ILLUSTRATION:

[14]I started trying to teach my son to swim early on. It was a chore. A year or so old at the time, the little guy didn't like getting water in his face in the bathtub, much less this massive ocean of a pool he was staring at now. At first, "teaching him to swim" meant getting him to splash around a bit on the top step, and maybe putting his lips in the water enough to blow bubbles if he was feeling really brave.

Eventually I convinced him to walk around with me in the shallow end, with a death-grip around my neck of course. Once we mastered that, it was time for the Big Show— Jumping Off the Side. Fulfilling my God-given duty as a daddy, I lifted him out of the pool, stood him on the side, and said, "Come on, jump!"

I think at that moment, my one-year-old son wrote me off as a crazy man.

The look on his face, in about two seconds, went from confusion to dawning understanding, to amused rejection, to outright contempt. He frowned and said, "No. I go see Mommy." Again acting faithfully on my solemn responsibility as a father, I refused to surrender, chased him down, and eventually convinced him (with various bribes) to come back to the pool.

---

[14] GREG GILBERT, WHAT IS THE GOSPEL? (CROSSWAY, 2010), PP. 71-72.

And so we came to the moment of truth.

I jumped into the water again and stood in front of him with my arms outstretched, watching him bob up and down in his swimmy-diaper as one-year-olds do when they kind of want to jump, but not really. "Come on, kiddo," I said. "I'm right here. I'll catch you. I promise!" He looked at me half skeptically, did one more little wind-up, bouncing at the knees, and then fell into the pool with what was more a flop than a jump.

AND I CAUGHT HIM.

After that we were off to the races. "Doot 'gain, Daddy! Doot 'gain!" And so commenced half an hour of jump, catch, lift, reset, jump, catch, lift, reset.

When it was over, my wife and I started to worry that maybe our son had gotten a bit too comfortable with the water. What if he wandered out to the pool when no one was there with him? Would he remember all the times he'd safely jumped into the water and decide he had this pool thing whipped? Would he jump again?

Over the next few days we watched him around the pool, and what we saw both comforted me as a parent and touched me deeply as a father. Never once did my little boy think about jumping into the water—at least not unless I was standing underneath him with my arms out, promising to catch him. And then he would fly!

You see, despite all his apparent successes, my son's trust was never in his own ability to handle the water. It was in his father, and in his father's promise: "Come on kiddo. Jump. I promise I'll catch you."

1. AN EARNEST REQUEST

When he heard that Jesus was come out of Judaea into Galilee, he went unto him, and besought him that he would come down, and heal his son: for he was at the point of death. – John 4:47

2. A GENTLE REBUKE

Then said Jesus unto him, Except ye see signs and wonders, ye will not believe. – John 4:48

For the Jews require a sign, and the Greeks seek after wisdom. – 1 Corinthians 1:22

3. A DEFINITE PROMISE

The nobleman saith unto him, Sir, come down ere my child die. Jesus saith unto him, <u>Go thy way; thy son liveth</u>. And the man believed the word that Jesus had spoken unto him, and he went his way. – John 4:49-50

4. A BELIEVING ACT

Jesus saith unto him, Go thy way; thy son liveth. <u>And the man believed the word that Jesus had spoken unto him, and he went his way</u>. – John 4:50

Jesus saith unto him, Thomas, because thou hast seen me, thou hast believed: blessed are they that have not seen, and yet have believed. – John 20:29

Now faith is the substance of things hoped for, the evidence of things not seen. – Hebrews 11:1

He that hath received his testimony hath set to his seal that God is true. – John 3:33

He that believeth on the Son of God hath the witness in himself: he that believeth not God hath made him a liar; because he believeth not the record that God gave of his Son. – 1 John 5:10

5. A CONFIRMING EVIDENCE

And as he was now going down, his servants met him, and told him, saying, Thy son liveth. Then enquired he of them the hour when he began to amend. And they said unto him, Yesterday at the seventh hour the fever left him. So the father knew that it was at the same hour, in the which Jesus said unto him, Thy son liveth: and himself believed, and his whole house. – John 4:51-53

And, behold, this day I am going the way of all the earth: and ye know in all your hearts and in all your souls, that not one thing hath failed of all the good things which the LORD your God spake concerning you; all are come to pass unto you, and not one thing hath failed thereof.
– Joshua 23:14

15. THE POWERLESS MAN

John 5:1-15

ILLUSTRATION:

[15]When a mountain is in your way what do you do? Just ask Ramchandra Das, 53, who lives in Bihar, India. In order to access nearby fields for food and work, Das and his fellow villagers had to take a 4.3-mile trek around a mountain. Fed up with the obstacle, Das did something about it. With just a hammer and chisel, he cut a 33-foot-long, 13-foot-wide tunnel through a narrow area of the mountain. It took Das fourteen years to complete the task. And get this: Das isn't the first person to do such a thing. He was inspired by another villager who cut a 393 feet-long, 33 feet-wide, 26 feet-high passage through another mountain so that villagers could reach a local hospital. That man was motivated to do so when his wife died because he was unable to get her to the hospital.

Jesus came across a man who was determined to get well, but found he was powerless to do so on his own.

1. SORROWFUL CONDITION

And a certain man was there, which had an infirmity thirty and eight years. – John 5:5

---

[15] RANDEEP RAMESH, "INDIAN VILLAGER TAKES 14 YEARS TO DIG TUNNEL THROUGH MOUNTAIN," GUARDIAN.CO.UK (12-1-09)

Afterward Jesus findeth him in the temple, and said unto him, Behold, thou art made whole: sin no more, lest a worse thing come unto thee. – John 5:14

2. FRUITLESS EFFORT

The impotent man answered him, Sir, I have no man, when the water is troubled, to put me into the pool: but while I am coming, another steppeth down before me. – John 5:7

3. MERCIFUL DELIVERER

When Jesus saw him lie, and knew that he had been now a long time in that case, he saith unto him, Wilt thou be made whole? – John 5:6

When my spirit was overwhelmed within me, then thou knewest my path. In the way wherein I walked have they privily laid a snare for me. – Psalm 142:3

4. PERSONAL CALL

Jesus saith unto him, Rise, take up thy bed, and walk. – John 5:8

5. SUDDEN CHANGE

And immediately the man was made whole, and took up his bed, and walked: and on the same day was the sabbath. – John 5:9

6. FEARLESS TESTIMONY

Afterward Jesus findeth him in the temple, and said unto him, Behold, thou art made whole: sin no more, lest a worse thing come unto thee. The man departed, and told the Jews that it was Jesus, which had made him whole. – John 5:14-15

For with the heart man believeth unto righteousness; and with the mouth confession is made unto salvation. – Romans 10:10

Yea, a man may say, Thou hast faith, and I have works: shew me thy faith without thy works, and I will shew thee my faith by my works. – James 2:18

Nevertheless among the chief rulers also many believed on him; but because of the Pharisees they did not confess him, lest they should be put out of the synagogue: For they loved the praise of men more than the praise of God. – John 12:42-43

Whosoever therefore shall confess me before men, him will I confess also before my Father which is in heaven. But whosoever shall deny me before men, him will I also deny before my Father which is in heaven. – Matthew 10:32-33

16. I AND MY FATHER

John 5:17-43

ILLUSTRATION:

[16]On a cold winter day Gabriel Estrada, a high school senior in Twin Lakes, Wisconsin, did the unthinkable. When his 17-year-old girlfriend secretly gave birth to a baby boy on January 15, 2002, she dressed it and asked him to deliver it to a church. Instead, Gabriel wrapped the baby in a canvas bag and left him in a portable toilet in a nearby park to die. But against incredible odds the baby was saved.

According to police there was virtually no chance the infant would survive. Temperatures were well below freezing. Lack of snow meant the nearby sledding hill would not be frequented by kids. And the sanitation company's scheduled pick-up at the port-a-potty was days away.

Village of Twin Lakes police credit a father and son for saving the child's life. About 4 o'clock in the afternoon on January 16th a father (wishing to remain anonymous) and his young son stopped at the abandoned West Side Park in need of a bathroom. Hearing a whimpering sound coming from the port-a-potty, they knew something was wrong. They called 911 to report what they had discovered.

When Officer Randy Prudik responded to the call, he pulled the canvas bag from the outdoor toilet and raced to

---

[16] MILWAUKEE JOURNAL SENTINEL (1-7-02)

nearby Burlington Memorial Hospital where the baby received emergency treatment.

"There's no way he would have survived that," Prudik said. "That little guy had somebody watching over him."

As a testament to the boy's survival, the nurses at the hospital dubbed him William Grant: William for the will to live and Grant for not taking life for granted.

On a grander scale, another Father and Son rescue team intervened on behalf of doomed humanity.

1. JESUS WAS LOVED BY THE FATHER

For the Father loveth the Son, and sheweth him all things that himself doeth: and he will shew him greater works than these, that ye may marvel. – John 5:20

The Father loveth the Son, and hath given all things into his hand. – John 3:35

For God so loved the world, that he gave his only begotten Son, that whosoever believeth in him should not perish, but have everlasting life. – John 3:16

2. JESUS WAS SENT BY THE FATHER

And the Father himself, which hath sent me, hath borne witness of me. Ye have neither heard his voice at any time, nor seen his shape. – John 5:37

Jesus said unto them, If God were your Father, ye would love me: for I proceeded forth and came from God; neither came I of myself, but he sent me. – John 8:42

But when the fulness of the time was come, God sent forth his Son, made of a woman, made under the law. – Galatians 4:4

As thou hast sent me into the world, even so have I also sent them into the world. – John 17:18

3. JESUS CAME IN HIS FATHER'S NAME

I am come in my Father's name, and ye receive me not: if another shall come in his own name, him ye will receive. – John 5:43

For before these days rose up Theudas, boasting himself to be somebody; to whom a number of men, about four hundred, joined themselves: who was slain; and all, as many as obeyed him, were scattered, and brought to nought. After this man rose up Judas of Galilee in the days of the taxing, and drew away much people after him: he also perished; and all, even as many as obeyed him, were dispersed. – Acts 5:36-37

Believest thou not that I am in the Father, and the Father in me? the words that I speak unto you I speak not of myself: but the Father that dwelleth in me, he doeth the works. – John 14:10

4. JESUS SEEKS TO DO THE WILL OF HIS FATHER

I can of mine own self do nothing: as I hear, I judge: and my judgment is just; because I seek not mine own will, but the will of the Father which hath sent me. – John 5:30

Then said I, Lo, I come: in the volume of the book it is written of me, I delight to do thy will, O my God: yea, thy law is within my heart. – Psalm 40:7-8

Jesus saith unto them, My meat is to do the will of him that sent me, and to finish his work. – John 4:34

And he went a little further, and fell on his face, and prayed, saying, O my Father, if it be possible, let this cup pass from me: nevertheless not as I will, but as thou wilt. – Matthew 26:39

5. JESUS FOLLOWED HIS FATHER'S EXAMPLE

And therefore did the Jews persecute Jesus, and sought to slay him, because he had done these things on the sabbath day. But Jesus answered them, My Father worketh hitherto, and I work. Therefore the Jews sought the more to kill him, because he not only had broken the sabbath, but said also that God was his Father, making himself equal with God. Then answered Jesus and said unto them, Verily, verily, I say unto you, The Son can do nothing of himself, but what he seeth the Father do: for what things soever he doeth, these also doeth the Son likewise. – John 5:16-19

6. JESUS POSSESSES THE FATHER'S PREROGATIVE OF LIFE

For as the Father hath life in himself; so hath he given to the Son to have life in himself. – John 5:26

As the living Father hath sent me, and I live by the Father: so he that eateth me, even he shall live by me. – John 6:57

7. JESUS QUICKENS WHOM THE FATHER WILL

For as the Father raiseth up the dead, and quickeneth them; even so the Son quickeneth whom he will. – John 5:21

8. JESUS JUDGES IN THE FATHER'S PLACE

For the Father judgeth no man, but hath committed all judgment unto the Son. –John 5:22

And hath given him authority to execute judgment also, because he is the Son of man. – John 5:27

And he commanded us to preach unto the people, and to testify that it is he which was ordained of God to be the Judge of quick and dead. – Acts 10:42

That at the name of Jesus every knee should bow, of things in heaven, and things in earth, and things under the earth. – Philippians 2:10

9. JESUS CLAIMS EQUALITY WITH THE FATHER

That all men should honour the Son, even as they honour the Father. He that honoureth not the Son honoureth not the Father which hath sent him. – John 5:23

He that hateth me hateth my Father also. – John 15:23

Whosoever denieth the Son, the same hath not the Father: (but) he that acknowledgeth the Son hath the Father also. – 1 John 2:23

I and my Father are one. – John 10:30

17. CHRIST AND THE HUNGRY MULTITUDE

John 6:1-14

ILLUSTRATION:

[17]On August 31, 2005, FEMA (Federal Emergency Management Agency) regional director Marty Bahamonde emailed the FEMA director regarding the situation in New Orleans immediately following Hurricane Katrina. Bahamonde wrote: "Sir, I know that you know the situation is past critical. Here [are] some things you might not know. Hotels are kicking people out, thousands gathering in the streets with no food or water. Hundreds still being rescued from homes.

"There are dying patients at the DMAT [disaster medical assistance team] tent. Estimates are many will die within hours. Evacuation in process. Plans developing for dome evacuation, but hotel situation adding to problem. We are out of food and running out of water at the dome, plans in works to address the critical need.

"FEMA staff is OK and holding own. DMAT staff working in deplorable conditions. The sooner we can get the medical patients out, the sooner we can get them out.

"Phone connectivity impossible."

The director responded: "Thanks for update. Anything specific I need to do or tweak?"

The director's insensitive response is a mirror to our own. Matthew writes, *"But when he saw the multitudes, he was*

---

[17] *Chicago Tribune* (11-3-05)

moved with compassion on them, because they fainted, and were scattered abroad, as sheep having no shepherd. Then saith he unto his disciples, The harvest truly is plenteous, but the labourers are few; Pray ye therefore the Lord of the harvest, that he will send forth labourers into his harvest. – Matthew 9:36-38

And we say, "Thanks for the update. Anything specific we need to do or tweak?"

1. JESUS DESIRES THAT THEY SHOULD BE FED

When Jesus then lifted up his eyes, and saw a great company come unto him, he saith unto Philip, Whence shall we buy bread, that these may eat? – John 6:5

And Jesus went forth, and saw a great multitude, and was moved with compassion toward them, and he healed their sick. – Matthew 14:14

2. JESUS KNOWS WHERE THE SUPPLY IS TO COME FROM

And this he said to prove him: for he himself knew what he would do. – John 6:6

3. JESUS SEEKS THE THOUGHTFUL INTEREST OF HIS FOLLOWERS

When Jesus then lifted up his eyes, and saw a great company come unto him, he saith unto Philip, Whence shall we buy bread, that these may eat? – John 6:5

4. JESUS MAKES USE OF LITTLE GIFTS

There is a lad here, which hath five barley loaves, and two small fishes: but what are they among so many? – John 6:9

And Jesus took the loaves; and when he had given thanks, he distributed to the disciples, and the disciples to them that were set down; and likewise of the fishes as much as they would. – John 6:11

But God hath chosen the foolish things of the world to confound the wise; and God hath chosen the weak things of the world to confound the things which are mighty; And base things of the world, and things which are despised, hath God chosen, yea, and things which are not, to bring to nought things that are: That no flesh should glory in his presence. – 1 Corinthians 1:27-29

5. JESUS HIMSELF IS ALL-SUFFICIENT FOR THIS EMERGENCY

And Jesus took the loaves; and when he had given thanks, he distributed to the disciples, and the disciples to them that were set down; and likewise of the fishes as much as they would. – John 6:11

Commit thy way unto the LORD; trust also in him; and he shall bring it to pass. – Psalm 37:5

6. JESUS FEEDS THE HUNGRY THROUGH HIS OWN DISCIPLES

And Jesus took the loaves; and when he had given thanks, he distributed to the disciples, and the disciples to them that were set down; and likewise of the fishes as much as they would. – John 6:11

7. JESUS PROVIDES ENOUGH FOR ALL

And Jesus took the loaves; and when he had given thanks, he distributed to the disciples, and the disciples to them that were set down; and likewise of the fishes <u>as much as they would</u>. – John 6:11

Therefore they gathered them together, and filled twelve baskets with the fragments of the five barley loaves, which remained over and above unto them that had eaten. – John 6:13

And Jesus said unto them, I am the bread of life: he that cometh to me shall never hunger; and he that believeth on me shall never thirst. – John 6:35

And he is the propitiation for our sins: and not for ours only, but also for the sins of the whole world. – 1 John 2:2

18. WALKING ON WATER

John 6:16-21

ILLUSTRATION:

[18]A 2012 article about Americans' belief in miracles summarized the following statistics gathered from recent surveys:

- 55 percent of Americans are "certain" that miracles happen (a 20 percent increase from 1991)

- 80 percent believe that miracles "certainly" or "probably" occur.

- 42 percent of Americans with no religious affiliation believe in miracles (compared to 32 percent from 20 years ago). In other words, THE STRONGEST GAINS IN OPENNESS TO MIRACLES WERE REPORTED BY THOSE WHO ATTEND SERVICES INFREQUENTLY.

- 23 percent of respondents said they had witnessed a miraculous physical healing and 16 percent said they had received a miraculous healing.

- 75 percent of respondents said they had prayed to God to receive healing from an illness or injury; nearly 85 percent had prayed for someone else's healing.

The author of the article concluded that the increasing openness to miracles "is not being driven by any one

---

[18] DAVID BRIGGS, "BELIEF IN MIRACLES CLIMBS IN THE AGE OF OPRAH," *Association of Religion Data Archives* (10-27-12)

generation, but seems to be more of a cultural shift ....
There's still a profound interest in spiritual things .... [As
Americans in general] we are not in this uniform march
toward secularism."

1. A CONSCIOUS NEED

*And entered into a ship, and went over the sea toward
Capernaum. And it was now dark, and Jesus was not come
to them. And the sea arose by reason of a great wind that
blew.* – John 6:17-18

2. A GREAT DISCOVERY

*So when they had rowed about five and twenty or thirty
furlongs, they see Jesus walking on the sea, and drawing
nigh unto the ship: and they were afraid.* – John 6:19

3. A COMFORTING MESSAGE

But he saith unto them, It is I; be not afraid. – John 6:20

4. A WILLING RECEPTION

*Then they willingly received him into the ship: and
immediately the ship was at the land whither they went.* –
John 6:21

5. AN IMMEDIATE RESULT

*Then they willingly received him into the ship: and
immediately the ship was at the land whither they went.* –
John 6:21

19. THE IMPERISHABLE FOOD

John 6:26-29

ILLUSTRATION:

[19]Often people have the idea that the image of Christ is something alien to human beings, something strange that God wants to add on to our life, something imposed upon us from outside that doesn't really fit us. In reality, however, the image of Christ is the fulfillment of the deepest hungers of the human heart for wholeness. The greatest thirst of our being is for fulfillment in Christ's image. The most profound yearning of the human spirit, which we try to fill with all sorts of inadequate substitutes, is the yearning for our completeness in the image of Christ.

1. DISAPPOINTING WORK

Labour not for the meat which perisheth, but for that meat which endureth unto everlasting life, which the Son of man shall give unto you: for him hath God the Father sealed. – John 6:27

Wherefore do ye spend money for that which is not bread? and your labour for that which satisfieth not? hearken diligently unto me, and eat ye that which is good, and let your soul delight itself in fatness. – Isaiah 55:2

---

[19] M. ROBERT MULHOLLAND JR. *Invitation to a Journey* (IVP, 1993), P. 34

And I will say to my soul, Soul, thou hast much goods laid up for many years; take thine ease, eat, drink, and be merry. – Luke 12:19

2. SATISFYING WORK

Labour not for the meat which perisheth, <u>but for that meat which endureth unto everlasting life</u>, which the Son of man shall give unto you: for him hath God the Father sealed. – John 6:27

1. It's **Suitable**.

I am the living bread which came down from heaven: if any man eat of this bread, he shall live for ever: and the bread that I will give is my flesh, which I will give for the life of the world. – John 6:51

2. It's **Stable**.

"<u>that meat which</u> endureth." (John 6:27b)

3. It's **Satisfying**.

And Jesus said unto them, I am the bread of life: he that cometh to me shall never hunger; and he that believeth on me shall never thirst. – John 6:35

3. INSPIRING WORK

Jesus answered and said unto them, This is the work of God, that ye believe on him whom he hath sent. – John 6:29

And this is his commandment, That we should believe on the name of his Son Jesus Christ, and love one another, as he gave us commandment. – 1 John 3:23

20. THE TRUE BREAD

John 6:30-40

ILLUSTRATION:

[20]Two years ago, a woman in my audience wrote to invite me to visit her, if I could. A few weeks ago, I was in her home city, along with my teammate and my wife. The woman was suffering from AIDS and by that time was dying. She had come here two years ago knowing she had AIDS. She hungered for something more than she had found in life. She had found Christ and came here for the deeper teaching and enrichment.

When we walked into her apartment, she was absolutely surprised. I'll never forget her expression. Her mom and dad stood next to her with a friend. She looked like a bag of just bones--a pathetic sight. She muttered words of gratitude that we had come. We spoke with her and prayed with her. When I turned to leave, I noticed a book on her table: THE HUNGER FOR SIGNIFICANCE by R. C. Sproul. In her loneliest moment, her greatest hunger was being filled, her hunger for significance. That's what our faith in Christ can do. People are able to endure life's unavoidable passages. Today she is with her Lord.

1. SOURCE OF THIS BREAD

Then Jesus said unto them, Verily, verily, I say unto you, Moses gave you not that bread from heaven; but my Father giveth you the true bread from heaven. – John 6:32

---

[20] RAVI ZACHARIAS, "IF THE FOUNDATIONS BE DESTROYED," PREACHING TODAY, TAPE NO. 142.

For <u>I came down from heaven</u>, not to do mine own will, but the will of him that sent me. – John 6:38

2. FORM OF THIS BREAD

And Jesus said unto them, <u>I am the bread of life</u>: he that cometh to me shall never hunger; and he that believeth on me shall never thirst. – John 6:35

And when the children of Israel saw it, they said one to another, It is manna: for they wist not what it was. And Moses said unto them, This is the bread which the LORD hath given you to eat. – Exodus 16:15

Having therefore, brethren, boldness to enter into the holiest by the blood of Jesus, By a new and living way, which he hath consecrated for us, through the veil, that is to say, <u>his flesh</u>. – Hebrews 10:19-20

3. NATURE OF THIS BREAD

Then Jesus said unto them, Verily, verily, I say unto you, Moses gave you not that bread from heaven; but my Father giveth you the true <u>bread from heaven</u>. For the bread of God is he which cometh down from heaven, and giveth life unto the world. – John 6:32-33

The LORD possessed me in the beginning of his way, before his works of old. I was set up from everlasting, from the beginning, or ever the earth was. When there were no depths, I was brought forth; when there were no fountains abounding with water. Before the mountains were settled, before the hills was I brought forth: While as yet he had not made the earth, nor the fields, nor the highest part of the dust of the world. When he prepared the heavens, I was there: when he set a compass upon the face of the depth: When he established the clouds above: when he strengthened the fountains of the deep: When he gave to the sea his decree, that the waters should not pass his commandment: when he appointed the foundations of the earth: Then I was by him, as one brought up with him: and I was daily his delight, rejoicing always before him. – Proverbs 8:22-30

4. PURPOSE OF THIS BREAD

For the bread of God is he which cometh down from heaven, and giveth life unto the world. – John 6:33

5. SATISFACTION OF THIS BREAD

And Jesus said unto them, I am the bread of life: he that cometh to me shall never hunger; and he that believeth on me shall never thirst. – John 6:35

21. THE PROHIBITED AND THE INVITED

John 7:32-39

ILLUSTRATION:

[21]The promise of a future inheritance is one of the many promises God makes to us in the Bible. But the concept itself is difficult for us to comprehend. One way to think about it would be to turn to some familiar names across the pond.

When Princess Diana died in 1997, she left a sizeable inheritance for her two sons, William and Harry, in the amount of $20.4 million. With investments and interest, that amount grew during their teens and twenties to $31.4 million. But the provision was such that William and Harry were only able to inherit this considerable estate after their 30th birthdays. In June 2012, William turned 30 and inherited his portion. Harry will inherit his portion on his 30th birthday as well. The estate is theirs. It is has been promised to them. It is in THEIR names, and it has been set aside for THEM.

In the same way, as followers of Christ, we have an inheritance. Based on Jesus' promise, it is ours. It's in your name, and it's set aside for you. At the right time, you too will receive your inheritance in full.

1. THE PROHIBITION

---

[21] FRANK LOVELACE, "PRINCE WILLIAM TURNS 30, INHERITS SHARE OF DIANA ESTATE," *Newsday* (6-20-12)

Then cried Jesus in the temple as he taught, saying, Ye both know me, and ye know whence I am: and I am not come of myself, but he that sent me is true, whom ye know not. – John 7:28

Ye shall seek me, and <u>shall not find me</u>: and <u>where I am, thither ye cannot come</u>. – John 7:34

2. THE INVITATION

In the last day, that great day of the feast, Jesus stood and cried, saying, <u>If any man thirst, let him come unto me, and drink</u>. – John 7:37

Jesus saith unto them, Come and dine. And none of the disciples durst ask him, Who art thou? knowing that it was the Lord. – John 21:12

3. THE PROMISE

My sheep hear my voice, and I know them, and they follow me: And I give unto them eternal life; and they shall never perish, neither shall any man pluck them out of my hand. – John 10:27-28

And the Spirit and the bride say, Come. And let him that heareth say, Come. And let him that is athirst come. And whosoever will, let him take the water of life freely. – Revelation 22:17

22. LAW AND GRACE

John 8:1-11

ILLUSTRATION:

[22]In his book What Good Is God?, Philip Yancey writes about being invited to speak at a conference on ministry to women in prostitution. After some discussion with his wife, Yancey agreed to accept the invitation as long as he could have the opportunity to question the women and hear their stories.

At the end of the conference Yancey had the following conversation with the women:

I had time for one more question. "Did you know that Jesus referred to your profession? Let me read you what he said: 'I tell you the truth, the tax collectors and the prostitutes are entering the kingdom of God ahead of you.' He was speaking to the religious authorities of his day. What do you think Jesus meant? Why did he single out prostitutes?"

After several minutes of silence a young woman from Eastern Europe spoke up in her broken English. "Everyone, she has someone to look down on. Not us. We are at the low. Our families, they feel shame for us. No mother nowhere looks at her little girl and says, 'Honey, when you grow up I want you be good prostitute.' Most places, we are breaking the law. Believe me, we know how people feel about us. People call us names: whore, slut,

---

[22] FROM What Good Is God?, BY PHILIP YANCEY, P. 75

hooker, harlot. We feel it too. We are the bottom. And sometimes when you are at the low, you cry for help. So when Jesus comes, we respond. Maybe Jesus meant that."

1. A SINNER UNDER THE LAW

Jesus went unto the mount of Olives. And early in the morning he came again into the temple, and all the people came unto him; and he sat down, and taught them. And the scribes and Pharisees brought unto him a woman taken in adultery; and when they had set her in the midst, They say unto him, Master, this woman was taken in adultery, in the very act. Now Moses in the law commanded us, that such should be stoned: but what sayest thou? – John 8:1-5

2. A SINNER UNDER GRACE

1. **Mystery**.

This they said, tempting him, that they might have to accuse him. But Jesus stooped down, and with his finger wrote on the ground, as though he heard them not. – John 8:6

2. **Revelation**.

So when they continued asking him, he lifted up himself, and said unto them, He that is without sin among you, let him first cast a stone at her. – John 8:7

3. **Conviction**.

And they which heard it, <u>being convicted by their own conscience</u>, went out one by one, beginning at the eldest, even unto the last: and Jesus was left alone, and the woman standing in the midst. – John 8:9

4. **Confidence**.

And they which heard it, being convicted by their own conscience, went out one by one, beginning at the eldest, even unto the last: and <u>Jesus was left alone, and the woman standing in the midst</u>. – John 8:9

5. **Confession**.

When Jesus had lifted up himself, and saw none but the woman, he said unto her, Woman, where are those thine accusers? hath no man condemned thee? She said, No man, Lord. And Jesus said unto her, Neither do I condemn thee: go, and sin no more. – John 8:10-11

6. **Salvation**.

She said, No man, Lord. And Jesus said unto her, <u>Neither do I condemn thee: go, and sin no more</u>. – John 8:11

For God sent not his Son into the world to condemn the world; but that the world through him might be saved. – John 3:17

23. CHRIST'S TESTIMONY CONCERNING HIMSELF
John 8:12-30

ILLUSTRATION:

[23]In his book *Jesus Among Other Gods*, Ravi Zacharias tells the story about how God, the Master Weaver, sovereignly works to weave beauty into our lives as we respond to his will. During a trip to India, Zacharias noticed a father and son who were weaving some of the most beautiful Indian wedding saris in the world. Zacharias explains the background and then describes the scene:

The sari, of course, is the garment worn by Indian women. It is usually six yards long. Wedding saris are a work of art; they are rich in gold and silver threads, resplendent with an array of colors.

The place I was visiting was known for making the best wedding saris in the world. I expected to see some elaborate system of machines and designs that would boggle the mind. Not so! Each sari was being made individually by a father-and-son team. The father sat above on a platform two- to three-feet higher than the son, surrounded by several spools of thread, some dark, some shining.

The son did just one thing. At a nod, from his father, he would move the shuttle from one side to the other and back

---

[23] RAVI ZACHARIAS, *Jesus Among Other Gods* (ZONDERVAN, 2000), PP. 17-18

again. The father would gather some threads in his fingers, nod once more, and the son would move the shuttle again. This would be repeated for hundreds of hours, till you would begin to see a magnificent pattern emerging.

The son had the easy task—just to move at the father's nod. All along, the father had the design in mind and brought the threads together.

The more I reflect on my own life and study the lives of others, I am fascinated to see the design God has for each one of us ... if we would only respond to him.

1. HE WAS NOT OF THIS WORLD

And he said unto them, Ye are from beneath; I am from above: ye are of this world; I am not of this world. – John 8:23

2. HE IS THE LIGHT OF THE WORLD

Then spake Jesus again unto them, saying, I am the light of the world: he that followeth me shall not walk in darkness, but shall have the light of life. – John 8:12

And this is the condemnation, that light is come into the world, and men loved darkness rather than light, because their deeds were evil. – John 3:19

3. THE FATHER WAS WITH HIM

And yet if I judge, my judgment is true: for I am not alone, but I and the Father that sent me. – John 8:16

4. HE SPOKE THE THINGS WHICH HE LEARNED FROM THE FATHER

I have many things to say and to judge of you: but he that sent me is true; and I speak to the world those things which I have heard of him. – John 8:26

Then said Jesus unto them, When ye have lifted up the Son of man, then shall ye know that I am he, and that I do nothing of myself; but as my Father hath taught me, I speak these things. – John 8:28

I will raise them up a Prophet from among their brethren, like unto thee, and will put my words in his mouth; and he shall speak unto them all that I shall command him. – Deuteronomy 18:18

Henceforth I call you not servants; for the servant knoweth not what his lord doeth: but I have called you friends; for all things that I have heard of my Father I have made known unto you. – John 15:15

5. HE ALWAYS PLEASED THE FATHER

And he that sent me is with me: the Father hath not left me alone; for I do always those things that please him. – John 8:29

6. TO KNOW HIM IS TO KNOW THE FATHER

Then said they unto him, Where is thy Father? Jesus answered, Ye neither know me, nor my Father: if ye had known me, ye should have known my Father also. – John 8:19

No man hath seen God at any time; the only begotten Son, which is in the bosom of the Father, he hath declared him. – John 1:18

7. TO DISBELIEVE HIM IS TO DIE IN SIN

I said therefore unto you, that ye shall die in your sins: for if ye believe not that I am he, ye shall die in your sins. – John 8:24

Jesus answered and said unto him, Verily, verily, I say unto thee, Except a man be born again, he cannot see the kingdom of God. – John 3:3

He that rejecteth me, and receiveth not my words, hath one that judgeth him: the word that I have spoken, the same shall judge him in the last day. – John 12:48

See that ye refuse not him that speaketh. For if they escaped not who refused him that spake on earth, much more shall not we escape, if we turn away from him that speaketh from heaven. – Hebrews 12:25

24. CHRIST'S HEART-SEARCHING "IFS"

John 8:31-54

ILLUSTRATION:

[24]In the last days of the Civil War, the Confederate capital, Richmond, Virginia, fell to the Union army. Abraham Lincoln insisted on visiting the city. Even though no one knew he was coming, slaves recognized him immediately and thronged around him. He had liberated them by the Emancipation Proclamation, and now Lincoln's army had set them free. According to Admiral David Porter, an eyewitness, Lincoln spoke to the throng around him:

"My poor friends, you are free—free as air. You can cast off the name of slave and trample upon it .... Liberty is your birthright."

But Lincoln also warned them not to abuse their freedom. "Let the world see that you merit [your freedom]," Lincoln said, "Don't let your joy carry you into excesses. Learn the laws and obey them."

That is very much like the message Jesus gives to those whom he has liberated by his death and resurrection. Jesus gives us our true birthright—spiritual freedom. But that freedom isn't an excuse for disobedience; it forms the basis for learning and obeying God's laws.

1. THE "IF" OF DISCIPLESHIP

---

[24] JAMES L. SWANSON, *Bloody Crimes* (WILLIAM MORROW, 2010), P.46

Then said Jesus to those Jews which believed on him, If ye continue in my word, then are ye my disciples indeed. – John 8:31

But he that received the seed into stony places, the same is he that heareth the word, and anon with joy receiveth it; Yet hath he not root in himself, but dureth for a while: for when tribulation or persecution ariseth because of the word, by and by he is offended. – Matthew 13:20-21

Now the just shall live by faith: but if any man draw back, my soul shall have no pleasure in him. – Hebrews 10:38

2. THE "IF" OF FREEDOM

If the Son therefore shall make you free, ye shall be free indeed. – John 8:36

For as many as are of the works of the law are under the curse: for it is written, Cursed is every one that continueth not in all things which are written in the book of the law to do them. – Galatians 3:10

Who shall lay any thing to the charge of God's elect? It is God that justifieth. – Romans 8:33

For sin shall not have dominion over you: for ye are not under the law, but under grace. – Romans 6:14

And deliver them who through fear of death were all their lifetime subject to bondage. – Hebrews 2:15

And they called them, and commanded them not to speak at all nor teach in the name of Jesus. But Peter and John answered and said unto them, Whether it be right in the sight of God to hearken unto you more than unto God, judge ye. For we cannot but speak the things which we have seen and heard. – Acts 4:18-20

3. THE "IF" OF SERVICE

They answered and said unto him, Abraham is our father. Jesus saith unto them, If ye were Abraham's children, ye would do the works of Abraham. – John 8:39

Know ye therefore that they which are of faith, the same are the children of Abraham. – Galatians 3:7

4. THE "IF" OF SONSHIP

Jesus said unto them, If God were your Father, ye would love me: for I proceeded forth and came from God; neither came I of myself, but he sent me. – John 8:42

Jesus saith unto him, I am the way, the truth, and the life: no man cometh unto the Father, but by me. – John 14:6

Whosoever believeth that Jesus is the Christ is born of God: and every one that loveth him that begat loveth him also that is begotten of him. – 1 John 5:1

5. THE "IF" OF RESPONSIBILITY

Which of you convinceth me of sin? And if I say the truth, why do ye not believe me? – John 8:46

Then spake Jesus again unto them, saying, I am the light of the world: he that followeth me shall not walk in darkness, but shall have the light of life. The Pharisees therefore said unto him, Thou bearest record of thyself; thy record is not true. Jesus answered and said unto them, Though I bear record of myself, yet my record is true: for I know whence I came, and whither I go; but ye cannot tell whence I come, and whither I go. Ye judge after the flesh; I judge no man. And yet if I judge, my judgment is true: for I am not alone, but I and the Father that sent me. It is also written in your law, that the testimony of two men is true. I am one that bear witness of myself, and the Father that sent me beareth witness of me. Then said they unto him, Where is thy Father? Jesus answered, Ye neither know me, nor my Father: if ye had known me, ye should have known my Father also. These words spake Jesus in the treasury, as he taught in the temple: and no man laid hands on him; for his hour was not yet come. Then said Jesus again unto them, I go my way, and ye shall seek me, and shall die in your sins: whither I go, ye cannot come. Then said the Jews, Will he kill himself? because he saith, Whither I go, ye cannot come. And he said unto them, Ye are from beneath; I am from above: ye are of this world; I am not of this world. I said therefore unto you, that ye shall die in your sins: for if ye believe not that I am he, ye shall die in your sins. – John 8:12-24

6. THE "IF" OF ASSURANCE

Verily, verily, I say unto you, If a man keep my saying, he shall never see death. – John 8:51

And whosoever liveth and believeth in me shall never die. Believest thou this? – John 11:26

For the wages of sin is death; but the gift of God is eternal life through Jesus Christ our Lord. – Romans 6:23

25. FROM DARKNESS TO LIGHT

John 9

ILLUSTRATION:

[25]Imagine eating at a restaurant devoid of light. Hard as it is to believe, some people are choosing to dine that way. Following a growing trend, sightless restaurants are opening up across Europe. What is a sightless restaurant? John Bohannon experienced it firsthand. Bohannon plunged into the "inky blackness of Unsicht-Bar, a restaurant named for the German word for invisible." To get to his table, it was necessary to place his hand on the shoulder of Magid the waiter, then allow his dining partner to put her hand on his shoulder. In single file, they carefully maneuvered to their chairs, with the waiter as their guide. Magid needed no light. Like most waiters in these restaurants, he is blind.

Bohannon felt panicked by the utter darkness and the inability to see his own hand while waving it in front of his face. He heard a glass crash to the floor from a nearby table. The reaction was "more desperate than the situation would merit under normal (well-lit) circumstances."

Since no lights of any kind are allowed in the dining room, a staff member must lead patrons to a candlelit bathroom when the need arises. Bohannon's unease over the situation began to build to the point where he wanted someone to lead him to the bathroom, just so he could see something

---

[25] "THE BEST FOOD I'VE TASTED BUT NEVER SEEN," *The Christian Science Monitor* (10-13-04)

again. He pushed aside the nervousness when Magid arrived with the food and Bohannon soon discovered the difficulties of using a fork you can't see.

At the end of this unique dining experience, the waiter arrived to lead Bohannon and his guest back out of the restaurant and into the light.

Whatever the pluses or minuses of sightless dining, one thing is clear. When choosing darkness over light, your best guide is blind.

1. BLINDNESS

And as Jesus passed by, he saw a man which was blind from his birth. – John 9:1

And Jesus answering said unto them, Suppose ye that these Galilaeans were sinners above all the Galilaeans, because they suffered such things? – Luke 13:2

When Jesus heard that, he said, This sickness is not unto death, but for the glory of God, that the Son of God might be glorified thereby. – John 11:4

2. DELIVERANCE

And said unto him, Go, wash in the pool of Siloam, (which is by interpretation, Sent.) He went his way therefore, and washed, and came seeing. – John 9:7

Then spake Jesus again unto them, saying, I am the light of the world: he that followeth me shall not walk in darkness, but shall have the light of life. – John 8:12

3. CONFESSION

The neighbours therefore, and they which before had seen him that he was blind, said, Is not this he that sat and begged? Some said, This is he: others said, He is like him: but he said, I am he. Therefore said they unto him, How were thine eyes opened? He answered and said, A man that is called Jesus made clay, and anointed mine eyes, and said unto me, Go to the pool of Siloam, and wash: and I went and washed, and I received sight. Then said they unto him, Where is he? He said, I know not. – John 9:8-12

4. ASSURANCE

He answered and said, Whether he be a sinner or no, I know not: one thing I know, that, whereas I was blind, now I see. – John 9:25

For we are not as many, which corrupt the word of God: but as of sincerity, but as of God, in the sight of God speak we in Christ. – 2 Corinthians 2:17

5. TESTIMONY

They say unto the blind man again, What sayest thou of him, that he hath opened thine eyes? He said, He is a prophet. – John 9:17

He answered them, I have told you already, and ye did not hear: wherefore would ye hear it again? will ye also be his disciples? – John 9:27

If this man were not of God, he could do nothing. – John 9:33

6. PERSECUTION

Then they reviled him, and said, Thou art his disciple; but we are Moses' disciples. – John 9:28

They answered and said unto him, Thou wast altogether born in sins, and dost thou teach us? And they cast him out. – John 9:34

Blessed are ye, when men shall hate you, and when they shall separate you from their company, and shall reproach you, and cast out your name as evil, for the Son of man's sake. – Luke 6:22

7. SATISFACTION

Jesus heard that they had cast him out; and when he had found him, he said unto him, Dost thou believe on the Son of God? He answered and said, Who is he, Lord, that I might believe on him? And Jesus said unto him, Thou hast both seen him, and it is he that talketh with thee. And he said, Lord, I believe. And he worshipped him. – John 9:35-38

Hear the word of the LORD, ye that tremble at his word; Your brethren that hated you, that cast you out for my name's sake, said, Let the LORD be glorified: but he shall appear to your joy, and they shall be ashamed. – Isaiah 66:5

8. JUDGMENT

And Jesus said, For judgment I am come into this world, that they which see not might see; and that they which see might be made blind. And some of the Pharisees which were with him heard these words, and said unto him, Are we blind also? Jesus said unto them, If ye were blind, ye should have no sin: but now ye say, We see; therefore your sin remaineth. – John 9:39-41

Then again called they the man that was blind, and said unto him, Give God the praise: we know that this man is a sinner. – John 9:24

Which of you convinceth me of sin? And if I say the truth, why do ye not believe me? – John 8:46

Let no man deceive himself. If any man among you seemeth to be wise in this world, let him become a fool, that he may be wise. – 1 Corinthians 3:18

26. THE SHEPHERD

John 10:1-10

ILLUSTRATION:

[26]In 1958, a U.S. soldier wandered the streets of Berlin to see the sights. Despite the bustling new life in parts of the city, reminders remained of the destruction of World War II. Walking through a residential area one evening, across the cobblestone street he saw an open space edged with flowers. In the center stood the stone front of what had been a church. The building was no longer there, but the rubble had been cleared away in an attempt to fill the empty space with a little park. The former church's main door was shaped in a Gothic arch, and over it was carved into the stone in German: HEAVEN AND EARTH WILL PASS AWAY BUT MY WORDS WILL NOT PASS AWAY.

As he stepped through the arch where the doors had once been, of course he wasn't inside anything. What was once a place of worship had been reduced to a patch of stone pavement and open sky. Not so with the Door--Jesus Christ! As we step into Christ, we enter into his unshakable, eternal presence. It cannot be reduced; it can only be experienced--forever.

1. THE SHEEPFOLD

Verily, verily, I say unto you, He that entereth not by the door into the sheepfold, but climbeth up some other way, the same is a thief and a robber. – John 10:1

---

[26] LEADERSHIP, VOL. 9, NO. 4.

2. THE ENTRANCE

Then said Jesus unto them again, Verily, verily, I say unto you, I am the door of the sheep. – John 10:7

Neither is there salvation in any other: for there is none other name under heaven given among men, whereby we must be saved. – Acts 4:12

I am the door: by me if any man enter in, he shall be saved, and shall go in and out, and find pasture. – John 10:9

3. THE GATEKEEPER

To him the porter openeth; and the sheep hear his voice: and he calleth his own sheep by name, and leadeth them out. – John 10:3

4. THE SHEPHERD

But he that entereth in by the door is the shepherd of the sheep. To him the porter openeth; and the sheep hear his voice: and <u>he calleth his own sheep by name</u>, and <u>leadeth them out</u>. And when he putteth forth his own sheep, <u>he goeth before them</u>, and the sheep follow him: for they know his voice. And a stranger will they not follow, but will flee from him: for they know not the voice of strangers. – John 10:2-5

1. Personal. *"He calleth his own sheep by name."*

2. Progressive. *"He leadeth them out."*

3. Exemplary. *"He goeth before them."*

In all things shewing thyself a pattern of good works: in doctrine shewing uncorruptness, gravity, sincerity. – Titus 2:7

Neither as being lords over God's heritage, but being ensamples to the flock. – 1 Peter 5:3

4. Protective. *"A stranger will they not follow..for they know not the voice of strangers."*

27. THE GOOD SHEPHERD

John 10:11-18

ILLUSTRATION:

[27]Cattle-rustling is a major problem in Uganda. The Ugandan army daily attempts to reunite cattle with their owners. The biggest difficulty lies in proving ownership. This article recounts how one elderly lady settled the issue:

The BBC's Nathan Etungu witnessed the process beginning in a village north of Mbale. He told the BBC's Network Africa that when an elderly woman stood before the herd a remarkable thing happened. She called her cows by name and to the amusement of the soldiers, as each cow heard her voice, it lifted its head and then followed her.

As far as the army was concerned, it was as strong a proof of ownership as one could find.

1. HE GIVES HIS LIFE FOR THE SHEEP

The thief cometh not, but for to steal, and to kill, and to destroy: I am come that they might have life, and that they might have it more abundantly. I am the good shepherd: the good shepherd giveth his life for the sheep. – John 10:10-11

Therefore doth my Father love me, because I lay down my life, that I might take it again. No man taketh it from me, but I lay it down of myself. I have power to lay it down,

---

[27] Paul Harvey, "UGANDAN COWS KNOW THEIR NAMES," BBC.COM, (2-25-03)

and I have power to take it again. This commandment have I received of my Father. – John 10:17-18

Now the God of peace, that brought again from the dead our Lord Jesus, that great shepherd of the sheep, through the blood of the everlasting covenant. – Hebrews 13:20

For ye were as sheep going astray; but are now returned unto the Shepherd and Bishop of your souls. – 1 Peter 2:25

2. HIS SHEEP HEAR HIS VOICE

And other sheep I have, which are not of this fold: them also I must bring, and they shall hear my voice; and there shall be one fold, and one shepherd. – John 10:16

And he is the propitiation for our sins: and not for ours only, but also for the sins of the whole world. – 1 John 2:2

3. HE KNOWS HIS SHEEP

I am the good shepherd, and <u>know my sheep</u>, and am known of mine. – John 10:14

But if any man love God, the same is known of him. – 1 Corinthians 8:3

4. HIS SHEEP KNOW HIM

I am the good shepherd, and know my sheep, and <u>am known of mine</u>. As the Father knoweth me, even so know I the Father: and I lay down my life for the sheep. – John 10:14-15

And we know that the Son of God is come, and hath given us an understanding, that we may know him that is true, and we are in him that is true, even in his Son Jesus Christ. This is the true God, and eternal life. – 1 John 5:20

For the which cause I also suffer these things: nevertheless I am not ashamed: for I know whom I have believed, and am persuaded that he is able to keep that which I have committed unto him against that day. – 2 Timothy 1:12

5. HIS SHEEP ARE OWNED BY HIM

But he that is an hireling, and not the shepherd, whose own the sheep are not, seeth the wolf coming, and leaveth the sheep, and fleeth: and the wolf catcheth them, and scattereth the sheep. – John 10:12

Take heed therefore unto yourselves, and to all the flock, over the which the Holy Ghost hath made you overseers, to feed the church of God, which he hath purchased with his own blood. – Acts 20:28

6. HE CARES FOR HIS SHEEP

The hireling fleeth, because he is an hireling, and careth not for the sheep. – John 10:13

Casting all your care upon him; for he careth for you. – 1 Peter 5:7

7. HIS SHEEP SHALL ALL BE GATHERED INTO ONE FLOCK

And other sheep I have, which are not of this fold: them also I must bring, and they shall hear my voice; and there shall be one fold, and one shepherd. – John 10:16

For the Lord himself shall descend from heaven with a shout, with the voice of the archangel, and with the trump of God: and the dead in Christ shall rise first: Then we which are alive and remain shall be caught up together with them in the clouds, to meet the Lord in the air: and so shall we ever be with the Lord. Wherefore comfort one another with these words. – 1 Thessalonians 4:16-18

28. THE SAFETY OF THE SHEEP

John 10:22-30

ILLUSTRATION:

[28]Bob, my father-in-law, hunts deer every fall in the mountains of north-central California. A number of farmers and ranchers in the area are willing to let individuals or small groups hunt on their property—if the hunters ask permission and show respect for the land. My father-in-law is one of the most congenial men I've ever met. It would take a surpassingly cranky landowner to turn him down.

Last year he approached a rancher and asked him if he might drive through a certain gate and do some hunting in the evening. When shadows lengthen and the October sun slips low in the west, deer begin to venture forth from their hiding places to graze.

The rancher gave Bob a thoughtful look and said, "Yeah, you can come on the land. But you'd better let me ride with you in the truck for awhile. Want to show you some things."

Now, I can imagine most men thinking, OH, COME ON! SHOW ME SOME THINGS? WHY DO I NEED A PASSENGER? EITHER LET ME IN OR TELL ME TO STAY OUT. I KNOW HOW TO DRIVE, AND I KNOW HOW TO HUNT. I'M A BIG BOY, AND I DON'T NEED A CHAPERONE!

---

[28] LARRY LIBBY, NO MATTER WHAT, NO MATTER WHERE (WATERBROOK PRESS, 2000), PP. 5-6

Bob, however, being the man he is, cheerfully assented, and the pair drove through the gate onto the ranch. They had been skimming across a wide, seemingly featureless field when the rancher suddenly said, "You'd better start slowing down."

Why? Had he seen a deer? Bob pulled his foot off the accelerator. But why stop? As far as he could see, there were no creeks, gullies, or fences. Just a wide pasture stretching out to the dusky foothills.

"Okay," said the rancher. "You'd better park right here. Want to show you something."

Bob did as he was told. They got out of the truck in the cool, mountain air and began walking. Then the rancher put his hand on Bob's shoulder and said, "Look up ahead."

My father-in-law walked slowly forward and then stopped dead in his tracks. Cleaving at right angles across their path—and across the pasture as far as he could see in both directions—was a yawning, black tear in the surface of the earth. Where they stood, the crack was probably 30 feet across. Peering over the edge, the hair on Bob's neck bristled.

WHERE WAS THE BOTTOM?

The sheer, rock-ribbed sides of the great volcanic fissure plunged to unknown depths. Cold, still air seemed to exhale from the blackness below....

Walking back to the truck, Bob marveled at how difficult it was to see the fissure from just yards away....

Bob smiled to himself. Having a guide wasn't such a bad thing! He gained a new appreciation for a man who knew the terrain—and where to park the truck.

Then came the Jews round about him, and said unto him, How long dost thou make us to doubt? If thou be the Christ, tell us plainly. Jesus answered them, I told you, and ye believed not: the works that I do in my Father's name, they bear witness of me. But ye believe not, because ye are not of my sheep, as I said unto you. – John 10:24-26

So we see that they could not enter in because of unbelief. – Hebrews 3:19

1. THEIR RELATIONSHIP

My sheep <u>hear my voice</u>, and I know them, and <u>they follow me</u>. – John 10:27

They are His by-

1. Sovereign Grace.

2. Deliberate Choice.

2. THEIR SECURITY

They are perfectly safe, because-

1. They have eternal life.

And I give unto them eternal life; and they shall never perish, neither shall any man pluck them out of my hand. – John 10:28

For the wages of sin is death; but the gift of God is eternal life through Jesus Christ our Lord. – Romans 6:23

2. They are the gift of the Father.

My Father, <u>which gave them me</u>, is greater than all; and no man is able to pluck them out of my Father's hand. – John 10:29

Elect according to the foreknowledge of God the Father, through sanctification of the Spirit, unto obedience and sprinkling of the blood of Jesus Christ: Grace unto you, and peace, be multiplied. – 1 Peter 1:2

All that the Father giveth me shall come to me; and him that cometh to me I will in no wise cast out. – John 6:37

Blessed be the God and Father of our Lord Jesus Christ, who hath blessed us with all spiritual blessings in heavenly places in Christ: According as he hath chosen us in him before the foundation of the world, that we should be holy and without blame before him in love: Having predestinated us unto the adoption of children by Jesus Christ to himself, according to the good pleasure of his will, To the praise of the glory of his grace, wherein he hath made us accepted in the beloved. – Ephesians 1:3-6

3. They are in Christ's hand.

And I give unto them eternal life; and they shall never perish, neither shall any man pluck them out of <u>my</u> hand. – John 10:28

That the saying might be fulfilled, which he spake, Of them which thou gavest me have I lost none. – John 18:9

4. They are in the Father's hand.

My Father, which gave them me, is greater than all; and no man is able to pluck them out of <u>my Father's hand</u>. – John 10:29

And the glory which thou gavest me I have given them; that they may be one, even as we are one. – John 17:22

I and my Father are one. – John 10:30

5. They have His promise.

And I give unto them eternal life; and <u>they shall never perish</u>, neither shall any man pluck them out of my hand. – John 10:28

29. LEARNING FROM LAZARUS

John 11

ILLUSTRATION:

[29]There is a school of thought in Christian circles that almost views death so much as a blessing that you are not allowed to cry .... [But in the Bible] death is an enemy, and it can be a fierce one .... It is ugly. It destroys relationships. It is to be feared. It is repulsive. There is something odious about death. Never pretend otherwise. But death does not have the last word .... Thank God for a Savior who could claim, "I am the resurrection and the life."

1. HIS SICKNESS

Now a certain man was sick, named Lazarus, of Bethany, the town of Mary and her sister Martha. – John 11:1

Therefore his sisters sent unto him, saying, Lord, behold, he whom thou lovest is sick. When Jesus heard that, he said, This sickness is not unto death, but for the glory of God, that the Son of God might be glorified thereby. – John 11:3-4

2. HIS DEATH

Then said Jesus unto them plainly, Lazarus is dead. – John 11:14

---

[29] D. A. CARSON, *Scandalous* (CROSSWAY, 2010), P. 133

For I was alive without the law once: but when the commandment came, sin revived, and I died. – Romans 7:9

3. HIS RESURRECTION

And he that was dead came forth, bound hand and foot with graveclothes: and his face was bound about with a napkin. Jesus saith unto them, Loose him, and let him go. – John 11:44

Verily, verily, I say unto you, Except a corn of wheat fall into the ground and die, it abideth alone: but if it die, it bringeth forth much fruit. – John 12:24

4. HIS LIBERTY

And he that was dead came forth, bound hand and foot with graveclothes: and his face was bound about with a napkin. Jesus saith unto them, <u>Loose him, and let him go</u>. – John 11:44

5. HIS COMMUNION

There they made him a supper; and Martha served: but Lazarus was one of them that sat at the table with him. – John 12:2

6. HIS TESTIMONY

Because that by reason of him many of the Jews went away, and believed on Jesus. – John 12:11

7. HIS SUFFERING

But the chief priests consulted that they might put Lazarus also to death. – John 12:10

If ye be reproached for the name of Christ, happy are ye; for the spirit of glory and of God resteth upon you: on their part he is evil spoken of, but on your part he is glorified. – 1 Peter 4:14

Yet if any man suffer as a Christian, let him not be ashamed; but let him glorify God on this behalf. – 1 Peter 4:16

30. DESCRIBING JESUS

John 11

ILLUSTRATION:

[30]Faith is confidence in the person of Jesus Christ and in his power, so that even when his power does not serve my end, my confidence in him remains because of who he is.

1. HIS DIVINITY

When Jesus heard that, he said, This sickness is not unto death, but for the glory of God, that the Son of God might be glorified thereby. – John 11:4

2. HIS LOVE

Now Jesus loved Martha, and her sister, and Lazarus. – John 11:5

3. HIS FAITH

Then after that saith he to his disciples, Let us go into Judaea again. His disciples say unto him, Master, the Jews of late sought to stone thee; and goest thou thither again? Jesus answered, Are there not twelve hours in the day? If any man walk in the day, he stumbleth not, because he seeth the light of this world. – John 11:7-9

---

[30] RAVI ZACHARIAS, *Jesus Among Other Gods* (THOMAS NELSON, 2002), P. 58

I must work the works of him that sent me, while it is day: the night cometh, when no man can work. – John 9:4

4. HIS JOY

And I am glad for your sakes that I was not there, to the intent ye may believe; nevertheless let us go unto him. – John 11:15

5. HIS INDIGNATION

When Jesus therefore saw her weeping, and the Jews also weeping which came with her, he groaned in the spirit, and was troubled. – John 11:33

6. HIS COMPASSION
Jesus wept. – John 11:35

For we have not an high priest which cannot be touched with the feeling of our infirmities; but was in all points tempted like as we are, yet without sin. – Hebrews 4:15

7. HIS POWER

And when he thus had spoken, he cried with a loud voice, Lazarus, come forth. And he that was dead came forth, bound hand and foot with graveclothes: and his face was bound about with a napkin. Jesus saith unto them, Loose him, and let him go. – John 11:43-44

When Christ, who is our life, shall appear, then shall ye also appear with him in glory. – Colossians 3:4

Now Jesus was not yet come into the town, but was in that place where Martha met him. – John 11:30

For our conversation is in heaven; from whence also we look for the Saviour, the Lord Jesus Christ: Who shall change our vile body, that it may be fashioned like unto his glorious body, according to the working whereby he is able even to subdue all things unto himself. – Philippians 3:20-21

Verily, verily, I say unto you, He that heareth my word, and believeth on him that sent me, hath everlasting life, and shall not come into condemnation; but is passed from death unto life. – John 5:24

31. A SUPPER SCENE

John 12:1-8

ILLUSTRATION:

[31] A young woman in England many years ago always wore a golden locket that she would not allow anyone to open or look into, and everyone thought there must be some romance connected with that locket and that in that locket must be the picture of the one she loved. The young woman died at an early age, and after her death the locket was opened, everyone wondering whose face he would find within. And in the locket was found simply a little slip of paper with these words written upon it, "Whom having not seen, I love." Her Lord Jesus was the only man she ever loved and longed for.

1. MARY, THE SACRIFICER

Then Jesus six days before the passover came to Bethany, where Lazarus was which had been dead, whom he raised from the dead. There they made him a supper; and Martha served: but Lazarus was one of them that sat at the table with him. Then took Mary a pound of ointment of spikenard, very costly, and anointed the feet of Jesus, and wiped his feet with her hair: and the house was filled with the odour of the ointment. – John 12:1-3

2. JUDAS, THE CRITICIZER

---

[31] R.A. TORREY IN A SERMON, "HOW TO BE SAVED" (*The Best of R.A. Torrey,* COMP. BY GEORGE B.T. DAVIS)

Then saith one of his disciples, Judas Iscariot, Simon's son, which should betray him, Why was not this ointment sold for three hundred pence, and given to the poor? This he said, not that he cared for the poor; but because he was a thief, and had the bag, and bare what was put therein. – John 12:4-6

3. JESUS, THE JUSTIFIER

Then said Jesus, Let her alone: against the day of my burying hath she kept this. For the poor always ye have with you; but me ye have not always. – John 12:7-8

Verily I say unto you, Wheresoever this gospel shall be preached throughout the whole world, this also that she hath done shall be spoken of for a memorial of her. – Mark 14:9

32. DEATH, LIFE, AND SERVICE

John 12:20-26

ILLUSTRATION:

[32]Professional golfer Paul Azinger was diagnosed with cancer at age 33. He had just won a PGA championship and had ten tournament victories to his credit.

He wrote, "A genuine feeling of fear came over me. I could die from cancer. Then another reality hit me even harder. I'm going to die eventually anyway, whether from cancer or something else. It's just a question of when. Everything I had accomplished in golf became meaningless to me. All I wanted to do was live."

Then he remembered something that Larry Moody, who teaches a Bible study on the tour, had said to him. "Zinger, we're not in the land of the living going to the land of the dying. We're in the land of the dying trying to get to the land of the living."

Golfer Paul Azinger recovered from chemotherapy and returned to the PGA tour. He's done pretty well. But that bout with cancer deepened his perspective. He wrote, "I've made a lot of money since I've been on the tour, and I've won a lot of tournaments, but that happiness is always temporary. The only way you will ever have true contentment is in a personal relationship with Jesus Christ. I'm not saying that nothing ever bothers me and I don't have problems, but I feel like I've found the answer to the six-foot hole."

---

[32] BOB RUSSELL, "RESURRECTION PROMISES," PREACHING TODAY, TAPE NO. 151.

1. DEATH

And there were certain Greeks among them that came up to worship at the feast: The same came therefore to Philip, which was of Bethsaida of Galilee, and desired him, saying, Sir, we would see Jesus. Philip cometh and telleth Andrew: and again Andrew and Philip tell Jesus. And Jesus answered them, saying, The hour is come, that the Son of man should be glorified. Verily, verily, I say unto you, <u>Except a corn of wheat fall into the ground and die, it abideth alone</u>: but if it die, it bringeth forth much fruit. – John 12:20-24

For we which live are alway delivered unto death for Jesus' sake, that the life also of Jesus might be made manifest in our mortal flesh. – 2 Corinthians 4:11

2. LIFE

Verily, verily, I say unto you, Except a corn of wheat fall into the ground and die, it abideth alone: <u>but if it die, it bringeth forth much fruit</u>. – John 12:24

Thou fool, that which thou sowest is not quickened, except it die. – 1 Corinthians 15:36

3. SERVICE

He that loveth his life shall lose it; and he that hateth his life in this world shall keep it unto life eternal. If any man serve me, let him follow me; and where I am, there shall also my servant be: if any man serve me, him will my Father honour. – John 12:25-26

Then said Jesus unto his disciples, If any man will come after me, let him deny himself, and take up his cross, and follow me. – Matthew 16:24

33. THE LIGHT OF THE WORLD

John 12:44-50

ILLUSTRATION:

[33]One weekend, author Paul Tripp gave his teenage son permission to spend the weekend at a friend's house. But during the weekend Paul received a call from the friend's mother, informing him that Paul's son was not at her home. (Her son had felt guilty about covering for Paul's son and confessed to his mom.) After Paul told his wife about their son's deception, Paul said, "Luella could feel my anger, and she said, 'I think you need to pray.' I said, 'I don't think I can pray for him right now.' She said, 'I didn't mean for you to pray for him; I think you need to pray for you.'"

Paul writes:

I went to my bedroom to pray for God's help, and it hit me that, because of his love, God had already begun a work of rescue in my son's life. God was the one who pressed in on the conscience of my son's friend, causing him to confess to his mom. God was the one who gave her the courage to make that difficult call to me. And God was the one giving me time to get a hold of myself before my son came home. Now, rather than wanting to rip into my son, I wanted to be part of what this God of grace was doing in this moment of rebellion, deception, hurt, and disappointment.

After giving his son a couple of hours to relax upon his return, Paul asked him if they could talk.

---

[33] PAUL DAVID TRIPP, *Forever: Why You Can't Live Without It* (ZONDERVAN, 2011), PP. 151-153

"Do you ever think about how much God loves you?" Paul asked his son.

"Sometimes," he answered.

"Do you ever think how much God's grace operates in your life every day?"

His son looked up but didn't speak.

"Do you know how much God's grace was working in your life even this weekend?"

"Who told you?" his son asked.

Paul said:

"You have lived your life in the light. You've made good choices. You've been an easy son to parent, but this weekend you took a step toward the darkness. You can live in the darkness if you want. You can learn to lie and deceive. You can use your friends as your cover ... You can step over God's boundaries. Or you can determine to live in God's light. I'm pleading with you: don't live in the darkness; live in the light."

"As I turned to walk away," Paul wrote, "I heard his voice from behind me saying, 'Dad, don't go.' As I turned around, with tears in his eyes, he said, 'Dad, I want to live in the light, but it's so hard. Will you help me?'"

1. THE ENTRANCE OF THE LIGHT

Jesus cried and said, He that believeth on me, believeth not on me, but on him that sent me. And he that seeth me seeth him that sent me. I am come a light into the world, that whosoever believeth on me should not abide in darkness. – John 12:44-46

2. THE NATURE OF THE LIGHT

For I have not spoken of myself; but the Father which sent me, he gave me a commandment, what I should say, and what I should speak. – John 12:49

And he that seeth me seeth him that sent me. – John 12:45

3. THE PURPOSE OF THE LIGHT

And if any man hear my words, and believe not, I judge him not: for I came not to judge the world, but to save the world. – John 12:47

For God sent not his Son into the world to condemn the world; but that the world through him might be saved. – John 3:17

4. THE RECEPTION OF THE LIGHT

I am come a light into the world, that <u>whosoever believeth on me should not abide in darkness</u>. – John 12:46

Nevertheless among the chief rulers also many believed on him; but because of the Pharisees they did not confess him, lest they should be put out of the synagogue: For they loved the praise of men more than the praise of God. – John 12:42-43

And this is the will of him that sent me, that every one which seeth the Son, and believeth on him, may have everlasting life: and I will raise him up at the last day. – John 6:40

5. THE REJECTION OF THE LIGHT

He that rejecteth me, and receiveth not my words, hath one that judgeth him: the word that I have spoken, the same shall judge him in the last day. –John 12:48

And this is the condemnation, that light is come into the world, and men loved darkness rather than light, because their deeds were evil. For every one that doeth evil hateth the light, neither cometh to the light, lest his deeds should be reproved. But he that doeth truth cometh to the light, that his deeds may be made manifest, that they are wrought in God. – John 3:19-21

34. CHRIST'S LAST TOKEN OF LOVE

John 13:1-17

ILLUSTRATION:

[34]The late Dawson Trotman, founder of The Navigators, was visiting Taiwan on one of his overseas trips. During the visit he hiked with a Taiwanese pastor back into one of the mountain villages to meet with some of the national Christians. The roads and trails were wet, and their shoes became very muddy. Later, someone asked this Taiwanese pastor what he remembered most about Dawson Trotman. Without hesitation the man replied, "He cleaned my shoes."

How surprised this humble national pastor must have been to arise in the morning and to realize that the Christian leader from America had arisen before him and cleaned the mud from his shoes. Such a spirit of servanthood marked Dawson Trotman throughout his Christian life. He died as he lived, actually giving his life to rescue someone else from drowning.

1. WHAT HE DID

He riseth from supper, and laid aside his garments; and took a towel, and girded himself. After that he poureth water into a bason, and began to wash the disciples' feet, and to wipe them with the towel wherewith he was girded.
– John 13:4-5

---

[34] JERRY BRIDGES, "LOVING BY SERVING," DISCIPLESHIP JOURNAL (MAY/JUNE 1985)

But made himself of no reputation, and took upon him the form of a servant, and was made in the likeness of men. – Philippians 2:7

Even as the Son of man came not to be ministered unto, but to minister, and to give his life a ransom for many. – Matthew 20:28

2. WHEN HE DID IT

Now before the feast of the passover, <u>when Jesus knew that his hour was come that he should depart out of this world</u> unto the Father, having loved his own which were in the world, he loved them unto the end. And supper being ended, the devil having now put into the heart of Judas Iscariot, Simon's son, to betray him; Jesus knowing that the Father had given all things into his hands, and that he was come from God, and went to God. – John 13:1-3

3. HOW HE DID IT

Now before the feast of the passover, when Jesus knew that his hour was come that he should depart out of this world unto the Father, <u>having loved his own which were in the world, he loved them unto the end</u>. – John 13:1

4. WHY HE DID IT

For I have given you an example, that ye should do as I have done to you. – John 13:15

Let nothing be done through strife or vainglory; but in lowliness of mind let each esteem other better than themselves. Look not every man on his own things, but every man also on the things of others. Let this mind be in you, which was also in Christ Jesus. – Philippians 2:3-5

Peter saith unto him, Thou shalt never wash my feet. Jesus answered him, If I wash thee not, thou hast no part with me. – John 13:8

35. SELF-EXCOMMUNICATED

John 13:21-30

ILLUSTRATION:

[35]Think of Judas. Judas decided to follow Jesus. Judas heard Jesus teach. He went out two by two with the others, healing the sick and exorcising demons. Judas did a lot of disciple kinds of things. Yet he is remembered solely for how his relationship with Jesus ended.

How a life, a ministry, or a relationship ends is absolutely crucial to everything that goes before it.

1. THE CAUSE OF CHRIST'S TROUBLE

When Jesus had thus said, he was troubled in spirit, and testified, and said, Verily, verily, I say unto you, that one of you shall betray me. – John 13:21

For he knew who should betray him; therefore said he, Ye are not all clean. – John 13:11

I speak not of you all: I know whom I have chosen: but that the scripture may be fulfilled, He that eateth bread with me hath lifted up his heel against me. – John 13:18

2. THE TOKEN OF CHRIST'S LOVE

---

[35] CRAIG BRIAN LARSON, "STRONG TO THE FINISH," PREACHING TODAY, TAPE NO. 155.

Jesus answered, He it is, to whom I shall give a sop, when I have dipped it. And when he had dipped the sop, he gave it to Judas Iscariot, the son of Simon. – John 13:26

3. THE DEPARTURE FROM CHRIST'S PRESENCE

He then having received the sop went immediately out: and it was night. – John 13:30

1. He went out from the best company on earth, into the company of God-hating, Christ-rejecting murderers.

2. He went out from the rule and service of the Son of God, into the rule and slavery of Satan.

3. He went out from the place of light and hope, into the night of darkness and despair.

4. He went out from the offer of eternal blessedness, into the place of eternal doom.

That he may take part of this ministry and apostleship, from which Judas by transgression fell, that he might go to his own place. – Acts 1:25

And ye will not come to me, that ye might have life. – John 5:40

36. A FANTASTIC FUTURE

John 14:1-4

ILLUSTRATION:

[36]Anne Graham Lotz, daughter of evangelist Billy Graham and his wife, Ruth, was interviewed on CNN in December of 2001. She was asked about those who died on September 11th. If they were not saved by accepting Christ, the reporters wanted to know, would they go to heaven? She replied:

In my little book, HEAVEN: MY FATHER'S HOUSE I tell about people who want to visit my father's home in western North Carolina. They drive up the long drive and come to the gate. They knock on the gate and say: "Billy Graham, let us in. We've read your books; we've watched you on TV; we've written to you; and we want to come to your house."

And my father says: "Depart from me, I don't know you. You're not a member of my family, and you've not made any arrangements to come."

But when I drive up that same driveway and knock on the gate, I say, "Daddy, this is Anne, and I've come home." The gate is thrown right open, and I go inside, because I'm the father's child.

Jesus said that heaven is his Father's house, speaking of God. Because heaven is God's house, he has the right to decide who comes in and who stays out. He says he will

---

[36] ANNE GRAHAM LOTZ, "FINDING MEANING IN SEPTEMBER 11," *cnn.com* (12-11-06)

welcome anyone inside his home, anyone can come, but they have to be born again into his family through faith in Jesus Christ.

That gives us a wonderful hope, that when the time comes—whether death comes as a thief in the night as it did for those in the [World Trade Center] towers, or comes as an angel of mercy after a long illness—we can be assured that at the end of the journey, we'll step right into our Father's arms. We'll be welcomed there, because we're our Father's child.

1. THE POWER OF CHRIST

Let not your heart be troubled: ye believe in God, believe also in me. – John 14:1

I and my Father are one. – John 10:30

And Jesus came and spake unto them, saying, All power is given unto me in heaven and in earth. – Matthew 28:18

2. THE MANY MANSIONS

In my Father's house are many mansions: if it were not so, I would have told you. I go to prepare a place for you. – John 14:2

3. THE PREPARED PLACE

In my Father's house are many mansions: if it were not so, I would have told you. I go to prepare a place for you. – John 14:2

4. THE COMING AGAIN

And if I go and prepare a place for you, <u>I will come again</u>, and receive you unto myself; that where I am, there ye may be also. – John 14:3

For the Lord himself shall descend from heaven with a shout, with the voice of the archangel, and with the trump of God: and the dead in Christ shall rise first: Then we which are alive and remain shall be caught up together with them in the clouds, to meet the Lord in the air: and so shall we ever be with the Lord. Wherefore comfort one another with these words. – 1 Thessalonians 4:16-18

For he must reign, till he hath put all enemies under his feet. – 1 Corinthians 15:25

5. THE GREAT RECEPTION

And if I go and prepare a place for you, I will come again, <u>and receive you unto myself</u>; that where I am, there ye may be also. – John 14:3

Father, I will that they also, whom thou hast given me, be with me where I am; that they may behold my glory, which thou hast given me: for thou lovedst me before the foundation of the world. – John 17:24

6. THE ETERNAL HOME

And if I go and prepare a place for you, I will come again, and receive you unto myself; that <u>where I am, there ye may be also</u>. – John 14:3

7. THE BLESSED ASSURANCE

And whither I go ye know, and the way ye know. – John 14:4

Jesus saith unto him, I am the way, the truth, and the life: no man cometh unto the Father, but by me. – John 14:6

37. CHRIST AND THE FATHER

John 14:6-21

ILLUSTRATION:

[37]There are two ways the Bible says you can get to heaven. Plan A is to earn it. That's the performance plan. And to earn it you only have to do this: never sin and always do what's right for the entire time that you live. Just be perfect.

Since none of us qualify for Plan A, God came up with Plan B, which is this: You trust Jesus Christ when he says, "I am the way, the truth and the life." He was the only perfect person who ever lived, because he was God. He came so we could know what God is like. And by trusting and establishing a relationship with him, you get in on his goodness.

My friend Ron Dunn took his young son to a carnival one time for his birthday. His son picked six boys to go with him, so Ron bought a roll of tickets. Every line he'd come up to, he'd pull off seven tickets and give them to all the kids. When they got to the Ferris wheel, all of a sudden there was this eighth little kid with his hand out.

Ron said, "Who are you?"

The kid said, "I'm Johnny."

Ron said, "Who are you, Johnny?"

---

[37] RICK WARREN, "WHAT DIFFERENCE DOES EASTER MAKE?" *Leadershipjournal.net* (4-10-06)

Johnny said, "I'm your son's new friend. And he said you would give me a ticket."

Ron asked me, "Do you think I gave him one? Absolutely."

1. HE DWELT IN THE FATHER

Believest thou not that I am in the Father, and the Father in me? the words that I speak unto you I speak not of myself: but the Father that dwelleth in me, he doeth the works. – John 14:10

No man hath seen God at any time. If we love one another, God dwelleth in us, and his love is perfected in us. Hereby know we that we dwell in him, and he in us, because he hath given us of his Spirit. And we have seen and do testify that the Father sent the Son to be the Saviour of the world. Whosoever shall confess that Jesus is the Son of God, God dwelleth in him, and he in God. And we have known and believed the love that God hath to us. God is love; and he that dwelleth in love dwelleth in God, and God in him. – 1 John 4:12-16

2. HIS FATHER DWELT IN HIM

Believe me that I am in the Father, and the Father in me: or else believe me for the very works' sake. – John 14:11

3. HE IS THE REVELATION OF THE FATHER

If ye had known me, ye should have known my Father also: and from henceforth ye know him, and have seen him. Philip saith unto him, Lord, shew us the Father, and it sufficeth us. Jesus saith unto him, Have I been so long time with you, and yet hast thou not known me, Philip? he that hath seen me hath seen the Father; and how sayest thou then, Shew us the Father? – John 14:7-9

4. HIS WORDS WERE THE WORDS OF THE FATHER

He that loveth me not keepeth not my sayings: and the word which ye hear is not mine, but the Father's which sent me. – John 14:24

Jesus answered them, and said, My doctrine is not mine, but his that sent me. – John 7:16

I have many things to say and to judge of you: but he that sent me is true; and I speak to the world those things which I have heard of him. They understood not that he spake to them of the Father. Then said Jesus unto them, When ye have lifted up the Son of man, then shall ye know that I am he, and that I do nothing of myself; but as my Father hath taught me, I speak these things. – John 8:26-28

5. HIS WORKS WERE THE WORKS OF THE FATHER

But that the world may know that I love the Father; and as the Father gave me commandment, even so I do. Arise, let us go hence. – John 14:31

If ye keep my commandments, ye shall abide in my love; even as I have kept my Father's commandments, and abide in his love. – John 15:10

Believe me that I am in the Father, and the Father in me: or else believe me for the very works' sake. – John 14:11

6. HIS DESIRE WAS THAT THE FATHER SHOULD BE GLORIFIED IN HIM

And whatsoever ye shall ask in my name, that will I do, that the Father may be glorified in the Son. – John 14:13

Hitherto have ye asked nothing in my name: ask, and ye shall receive, that your joy may be full. – John 16:24

7. HE IS THE WAY TO THE FATHER

Jesus saith unto him, I am the way, the truth, and the life: no man cometh unto the Father, but by me. – John 14:6

For through him we both have access by one Spirit unto the Father. – Ephesians 2:18

8. TO LOVE HIM IS TO BE LOVED OF THE FATHER

He that hath my commandments, and keepeth them, he it is that loveth me: and he that loveth me shall be loved of my Father, and I will love him, and will manifest myself to him. – John 14:21

If any man love not the Lord Jesus Christ, let him be Anathema Maranatha. – 1 Corinthians 16:22

38. LOVE'S REWARD

John 14:21-24

ILLUSTRATION:

[38]The true pupil, say of some great musician or painter, yields his master a wholehearted and unhesitating submission. In practicing his scales or mixing the colors, in the slow and patient study of the elements of his art, he knows that it is wisdom simply and fully to obey.

It is this wholehearted surrender to His guidance, this implicit submission to His authority, which Christ asks. We come to Him asking Him to teach us the lost art of obeying God as He did. ... The only way of learning to do a thing is to do it. The only way of learning obedience from Christ is to give up your will to Him and to make the doing of His will the one desire and delight of your heart.

1. THE PROMISE

Philip saith unto him, Lord, shew us the Father, and it sufficeth us. Jesus saith unto him, Have I been so long time with you, and yet hast thou not known me, Philip? he that hath seen me hath seen the Father; and how sayest thou then, Shew us the Father? – John 14:8-9

He that hath my commandments, and keepeth them, he it is that loveth me: and he that loveth me shall be loved of my Father, and I will love him, and will manifest myself to him. Judas saith unto him, not Iscariot, Lord, how is it that thou wilt manifest thyself unto us, and not unto the world?

---

[38] ANDREW MURRAY IN "WITH CHRIST IN THE SCHOOL OF OBEDIENCE."

Jesus answered and said unto him, If a man love me, he will keep my words: and my Father will love him, and we will come unto him, and make our abode with him. – John 14:21-23

Jesus saith unto her, Mary. She turned herself, and saith unto him, Rabboni; which is to say, Master. Jesus saith unto her, Touch me not; for I am not yet ascended to my Father: but go to my brethren, and say unto them, I ascend unto my Father, and your Father; and to my God, and your God. – John 20:16-17

Afterward he appeared unto the eleven as they sat at meat, and upbraided them with their unbelief and hardness of heart, because they believed not them which had seen him after he was risen. – Mark 16:14

And when he had so said, he shewed unto them his hands and his side. Then were the disciples glad, when they saw the Lord. Then said Jesus to them again, Peace be unto you: as my Father hath sent me, even so send I you. And when he had said this, he breathed on them, and saith unto them, Receive ye the Holy Ghost. – John 20:20-22

And after eight days again his disciples were within, and Thomas with them: then came Jesus, the doors being shut, and stood in the midst, and said, Peace be unto you. Then saith he to Thomas, Reach hither thy finger, and behold my hands; and reach hither thy hand, and thrust it into my side: and be not faithless, but believing. And Thomas answered and said unto him, My Lord and my God. – John 20:26-28

And the night following the Lord stood by him, and said, Be of good cheer, Paul: for as thou hast testified of me in Jerusalem, so must thou bear witness also at Rome. – Acts 23:11

Then spake the Lord to Paul in the night by a vision, Be not afraid, but speak, and hold not thy peace: For I am with thee, and no man shall set on thee to hurt thee: for I have much people in this city. – Acts 18:9-10

For there stood by me this night the angel of God, whose I am, and whom I serve, Saying, Fear not, Paul; thou must be brought before Caesar: and, lo, God hath given thee all them that sail with thee. – Acts 27:23-24

But he, being full of the Holy Ghost, looked up stedfastly into heaven, and saw the glory of God, and Jesus standing on the right hand of God. – Acts 7:55

2. THE CONDITION

Jesus answered and said unto him, If a man love me, he will keep my words: and my Father will love him, and we will come unto him, and make our abode with him. He that loveth me not keepeth not my sayings: and the word which ye hear is not mine, but the Father's which sent me. – John 14:23-24

His mother saith unto the servants, Whatsoever he saith unto you, do it. – John 2:5

The Revelation of Jesus Christ, which God gave unto him, to shew unto his <u>servants</u> things which must shortly come to pass; and he sent and signified it by his angel unto his servant John. – Revelation 1:1

39. FRUIT-BEARING

John 15:1-8

ILLUSTRATION:

[39]Stuart Briscoe, author and long-time pastor of Elmbrook Church in Brookfield, Wisconsin, tells the following story:

Many years ago, during the Cold War, I traveled to Poland for several weeks of itinerant ministry. One winter day my sponsors drove me in the dead of night to the middle of nowhere. I walked into a dilapidated building crammed with one hundred young people. I realized it was a unique opportunity.

Through an interpreter I preached from John 15 on abiding in Christ. Ten minutes into my message, the lights went out. Pitch black.

My interpreter urged me to keep talking. Unable to see my notes or read my Bible, I continued. After I had preached in the dark for twenty minutes, the lights suddenly blinked on, and what I saw startled me: everyone was on their knees, and they remained there for the rest of my message.

The next day I commented on this to one man, and he said, "After you left, we stayed on our knees most of the night. Your teaching was new to us. We wanted to make sure we were abiding in Christ."

Thou hast brought a vine out of Egypt: thou hast cast out the heathen, and planted it. – Psalm 80:8

---

[39] MARSHALL SHELLEY, *Changing Lives Through Preaching and Worship* (RANDOM HOUSE, 1995), P. 147

Yet I had planted thee a noble vine, wholly a right seed: how then art thou turned into the degenerate plant of a strange vine unto me? – Jeremiah 2:21

1. THE SOURCE OF FRUIT

Abide in me, and I in you. As the branch cannot bear fruit of itself, except it abide in the vine; no more can ye, except ye abide in me. I am the vine, ye are the branches: He that abideth in me, and I in him, the same bringeth forth much fruit: for without me ye can do nothing. – John 15:4-5

For he whom God hath sent speaketh the words of God: for God giveth not the Spirit by measure unto him. – John 3:34

Ephraim shall say, What have I to do any more with idols? I have heard him, and observed him: I am like a green fir tree. From me is thy fruit found. – Hosea 14:8

2. THE REMOVAL OF THE FRUITLESS

I am the true vine, and my Father is the husbandman. Every branch in me that beareth not fruit he taketh away: and every branch that beareth fruit, he purgeth it, that it may bring forth more fruit. – John 15:1-2

If a man abide not in me, he is cast forth as a branch, and is withered; and men gather them, and cast them into the fire, and they are burned. – John 15:6

3. THE PRUNING OF THE FRUITFUL

Every branch in me that beareth not fruit he taketh away: and <u>every branch that beareth fruit, he purgeth it, that it may bring forth more fruit</u>. Now ye are clean through the word which I have spoken unto you. – John 15:2-3

4. THE NATURE OF THE FRUIT

Herein is my Father glorified, <u>that ye bear much fruit</u>; so shall ye be my disciples. – John 15:8

And he shall be like a tree planted by the rivers of water, that bringeth forth his fruit in his season; his leaf also shall not wither; and whatsoever he doeth shall prosper. – Psalm 1:3

5. THE CONDITION OF FRUITFULNESS

Abide in me, and I in you. As the branch cannot bear fruit of itself, except it abide in the vine; no more can ye, except ye abide in me. – I am the vine, ye are the branches: He that abideth in me, and I in him, the same bringeth forth much fruit: for without me ye can do nothing. – John 15:4-5

40. BRANCHES, DISCIPLES, FRIENDS

John 15

ILLUSTRATION:

[40]During the Vietnam War, my uncle, Captain Ray Baker, flew for the Strategic Air Command. The Air Force trained him, along with all the other pilots, to run out of their barracks to their planes at the sound of a buzzer. He couldn't begin to remember how many times he had dropped his utensils during dinner and bolted to his bomber.

He then came home on a furlough to California.

When he arrived, we took him to his favorite Mexican restaurant. Everything was going great until Captain Baker jumped up without warning and ran out of the building into the parking lot.

Catching up with him when he finally stopped running, I asked him in total puzzlement, "Where were you going?"

"I was looking for my plane," was his bewildered reply as he searched the horizon for the B-52.

"But what prompted you to run out here?" I asked.

"I heard the buzzer," he said.

Then I realized that directly above our table was a buzzer the kitchen used to call the waiters to pick up their meals.

Obedience speaks of unquestioned, immediate action. Is this not what Jesus Christ wants from his followers?

---

[40] MARTIN BAKER, STOCKTON, CALIFORNIA

1. AS BRANCHES, WE RECEIVE

I am the vine, ye are the branches: He that abideth in me, and I in him, the same bringeth forth much fruit: for without me ye can do nothing. – John 15:5

Yet a little while, and the world seeth me no more; but ye see me: because I live, ye shall live also. – John 14:19

But the fruit of the Spirit is love, joy, peace, longsuffering, gentleness, goodness, faith, Meekness, temperance: against such there is no law. – Galatians 5:22-23

2. AS DISCIPLES, WE FOLLOW

If ye abide in me, and my words abide in you, ye shall ask what ye will, and it shall be done unto you. Herein is my Father glorified, that ye bear much fruit; so shall ye be my disciples. – John 15:7-8

Then said Jesus to those Jews which believed on him, If ye continue in my word, then are ye my disciples indeed. – John 8:31

By this shall all men know that ye are my disciples, if ye have love one to another. – John 13:35

3. AS FRIENDS, WE COMMUNE

Ye are my friends, if ye do whatsoever I command you. Henceforth I call you not servants; for the servant knoweth not what his lord doeth: but I have called you friends; for all things that I have heard of my Father I have made known unto you. – John 15:14-15

1. Sharers of His SECRETS.

The secret of the LORD is with them that fear him; and he will shew them his covenant. – Psalm 25:14

2. Sharers of His SUFFERINGS.

If the world hate you, ye know that it hated me before it hated you. If ye were of the world, the world would love his own: but because ye are not of the world, but I have chosen you out of the world, therefore the world hateth you. – John 15:18-19

3. Sharers of His CONSOLATIONS.

For as the sufferings of Christ abound in us, so our consolation also aboundeth by Christ. – 2 Corinthians 1:5

41. "I AND YOU"

John 15:12-26

ILLUSTRATION:

[41]Ever feel overwhelmed by the Bible's command to love unconditionally? When people ask me, "How can I ever start to love everyone like I should?" I give the same answer I give those who ask how they can start jogging: Start slow, and then get slower! For the first week, the goal is "just to keep moving." Too many people buy new shoes and a fancy running suit and sprint out the door, eagerly chugging as hard as they can for about three blocks. Then their stomachs begin to ache, their muscles cramp, and their lungs burn. They wind up hitchhiking home exhausted, and gasp, "I will never do that again." That's called anaerobic (without oxygen) running. It's caused by a body using up more oxygen than it takes in.

Many people try to run that way, and many people try to love that way. They love with great fervor and self-sacrifice, giving 100 percent but without the resources to continue for a lifetime. Down the road they find themselves in pain, gasping and cramped, saying, "I will never do that again." Love, like running, must be aerobic. Our output must be matched by our intake. Running requires oxygen.

An enduring love requires God's word, his consolation, his presence. As we love aerobically, we'll build up our capacity to do more and more. And pretty soon we won't

---

[41] ROGER THOMPSON, LEADERSHIP, VOL. 4, NO. 1.

be huffing and puffing for half a mile; we'll be running marathons.

1. GRACE

This is my commandment, That ye love one another, as <u>I have loved you</u>. – John 15:12

As the Father hath loved me, so have I loved you: continue ye in my love. – John 15:9

For ye know the grace of our Lord Jesus Christ, that, though he was rich, yet for your sakes he became poor, that ye through his poverty might be rich. – 2 Corinthians 8:9

2. SEPARATION

If ye were of the world, the world would love his own: but because ye are not of the world, but I have chosen you out of the world, therefore the world hateth you. – John 15:19

Not as Cain, who was of that wicked one, and slew his brother. And wherefore slew he him? Because his own works were evil, and his brother's righteous. – 1 John 3:12

3. FRIENDSHIP

Henceforth I call you <u>not servants</u>; for the servant knoweth not what his lord doeth: but <u>I have called you friends</u>; for all things that I have heard of my Father I have made known unto you. – John 15:15

4. TEACHING

Henceforth I call you not servants; for the servant knoweth not what his lord doeth: but I have called you friends; for <u>all things</u> that I have heard of my Father <u>I have made known unto you</u>. – John 15:15

5. RESPONSIBILITY

Ye have not chosen me, but <u>I have chosen you</u>, and <u>ordained you</u>, that <u>ye should go and bring forth fruit</u>, and that your fruit should remain: that whatsoever ye shall ask of the Father in my name, he may give it you. – John 15:16

6. BROTHERLY LOVE

These things I command you, that ye love one another. – John 15:17

Salt is good: but if the salt have lost his saltness, wherewith will ye season it? Have salt in yourselves, and have peace one with another. – Mark 9:50

7. PROMISE

But when the Comforter is come, whom I will send unto you from the Father, even the Spirit of truth, which proceedeth from the Father, he shall testify of me. – John 15:26

Even the Spirit of truth; whom the world cannot receive, because it seeth him not, neither knoweth him: but ye know him; for he dwelleth with you, and shall be in you. – John 14:17

42. THE GREAT HELPER

John 16:7-15

ILLUSTRATION:

[42]When I was a little boy, I used to be taken in the summer to the Northern coast of Scotland to see my mother's relatives. My mother had a cousin who had been grievously ill when he was just recently married at the age of 21, and he had become absolutely paralyzed. There was only one thing he could do with his body: he could move his head a bit, and if they put a cup of tea in his hand he could move the tea, and he could sip the tea. He used to sit in a wheelchair and from time to time he would make guttural noises: "Uuuuh … Uuuuh … Uuuuh." And after I got over the fright, the fear of the unknown, and the strange, I began to notice that every time these groans came from him, the woman he had married when he was 21 would appear by some, it seemed, mystical gift of interpretation, and give him exactly what he wanted.

That's how we are sometimes, we're paralyzed, and we don't know how to pray. And in this world, sometimes to this world, we seem insignificant and unimportant and to be passed by, and to be despised. But the Spirit helps us in our weakness.

Likewise the Spirit also helpeth our infirmities: for we know not what we should pray for as we ought: but the Spirit itself maketh intercession for us with groanings which cannot be uttered. – Romans 8:26

---

[42] THE MYSTERY OF THE THIRD GROANING -- SERMON BY SINCLAIR FERGUSON

1. THE CONDITION OF HIS COMING

Nevertheless I tell you the truth; It is expedient for you that I go away: for if I go not away, the Comforter will not come unto you; but if I depart, I will send him unto you. – John 16:7

Therefore being by the right hand of God exalted, and having received of the Father the promise of the Holy Ghost, he hath shed forth this, which ye now see and hear. – Acts 2:33

(But this spake he of the Spirit, which they that believe on him should receive: for the Holy Ghost was not yet given; because that Jesus was not yet glorified.) – John 7:39

2. HIS MISSION IN THE WORLD

And when he is come, he will reprove the world of sin, and of righteousness, and of judgment. – John 16:8

1. Of Sin.

Of sin, because they believe not on me. – John 16:9

2. Of Righteousness.

Of righteousness, because I go to my Father, and ye see me no more. – John 16:10

Who was delivered for our offences, and was raised again for our justification. – Romans 4:25

But of him are ye in Christ Jesus, who of God is made unto us wisdom, and righteousness, and sanctification, and redemption. – 1 Corinthians 1:30

3. Of Judgment.

Of judgment, because the prince of this world is judged. – John 16:11

He that believeth on him is not condemned: but he that believeth not is condemned already, because he hath not believed in the name of the only begotten Son of God. – John 3:18

And into whatsoever city ye enter, and they receive you, eat such things as are set before you. – Luke 10:8

3. HIS MISSION TO THE CHURCH.

1. A Guide into all Truth.

Howbeit when he, the Spirit of truth, is come, <u>he will guide you into all truth</u>: for he shall not speak of himself; but whatsoever he shall hear, that shall he speak: and he will shew you things to come. – John 16:13

But the anointing which ye have received of him abideth in you, and ye need not that any man teach you: but as the same anointing teacheth you of all things, and is truth, and is no lie, and even as it hath taught you, ye shall abide in him. – 1 John 2:27

2. A Revealer of the Things of Christ.

He shall glorify me: for he shall receive of mine, and shall shew it unto you. All things that the Father hath are mine: therefore said I, that he shall take of mine, and shall shew it unto you. – John 16:14-15

3. An Example of Self-Abandoned Service.

Howbeit when he, the Spirit of truth, is come, he will guide you into all truth: for <u>he shall not speak of himself; but whatsoever he shall hear, that shall he speak</u>: and he will shew you things to come. – John 16:13

Believest thou not that I am in the Father, and the Father in me? the words that I speak unto you <u>I speak not of myself: but the Father that dwelleth in me, he doeth the works</u>. – John 14:10

43. A LITTLE WHILE

John 16:16-23

ILLUSTRATION:

[43]Kelly James was a 48-year-old landscape architect who loved to climb mountains. On December 9 of 2006, he and two of his friends set out to climb Mount Hood in Welches, Oregon. Tragically, they were caught by a sudden blizzard after reaching the summit, and forced to take shelter in a snow cave. Kelly was able to use his cell phone to call his family and tell them what was going on, but the storm was too severe for rescue workers to operate. All three hikers eventually perished.

In an interview with Katie Couric on the CBS EVENING NEWS, Kelly's widow, Karen James, demonstrated the extreme faith in Jesus Christ that had defined life for the couple. During the interview, Couric asked if Karen was angry at all with her husband for choosing to climb in the first place. She replied: "I'm not angry. I'm really sad our journey is over, for a while, and I miss him terribly. But he loved life so much, and he taught me how to love. He taught me how to live. And I don't know how you can be angry at someone who loved their family, who loved God...and gave back so much more than he took."

When asked how her husband would like to be remembered, Karen referred to his faith in Jesus: "Kelly had this little ornament, and he's had it since he was little. It's a manger. It's just this little plastic thing. And it's always the tradition that [our son] Jack and Kelly put it on the tree together. And so I said this Christmas, 'We're

---

[43] "CLIMBER'S WIDOW TELLS HER STORY," *CBS Evening News* (12-21-06)

going to put that ornament on the tree.' And one of the things that we really understand about Christmas is that little baby born in a barn is the reason our family has so much strength now. And that is really important to Kelly."

Impressed by the strength of Karen's faith, Couric asked if the family's confidence in God had been tested by her husband's death. "No, it was never tested," Karen answered. "I remember one time we were watching TV, and Kelly said to me, 'I can't wait to go to heaven.' And I said, 'What?' We were watching some show that had nothing to do with it. And he said, 'Yeah, that's going to be really cool.' And I said, "Can you hold off? Can we wait?' But he wasn't scared. And so those conversations are what I hold on to."

To conclude, Couric asked Mrs. James if there were any lessons that could be

learned from her husband's tragedy. Karen replied: "I've told a colleague of mine that men should hold their wives really, really tight, because you don't know when our journey's going to end. My journey ended with an 'I love you.' And…for others, if their journey ends with an 'I love you,' it's a lot to hold onto."

1. IT'S HISTORICAL

A little while, and ye shall not see me: and again, a little while, and ye shall see me, because I go to the Father. Then said some of his disciples among themselves, What is this that he saith unto us, A little while, and ye shall not see me: and again, a little while, and ye shall see me: and, Because I go to the Father? They said therefore, What is this that he saith, A little while? we cannot tell what he saith. Now Jesus knew that they were desirous to ask him, and said unto them, Do ye enquire among yourselves of that I said, A little while, and ye shall not see me: and again, a little while, and ye shall see me? – John 16:16-19

And he said unto them, What manner of communications are these that ye have one to another, as ye walk, and are sad? – Luke 24:17

And when he had so said, he shewed unto them his hands and his side. Then were the disciples glad, when they saw the Lord. – John 20:20

2. IT'S PERSONAL

Verily, verily, I say unto you, That ye shall weep and lament, but the world shall rejoice: and ye shall be sorrowful, but your sorrow shall be turned into joy. – John 16:20

These things I have spoken unto you, that in me ye might have peace. In the world ye shall have tribulation: but be of good cheer; I have overcome the world. – John 16:33

3. IT'S DISPENSATIONAL

A woman when she is in travail hath sorrow, because her hour is come: but as soon as she is delivered of the child, she remembereth no more the anguish, for joy that a man is born into the world. And ye now therefore have sorrow: but I will see you again, and your heart shall rejoice, and your joy no man taketh from you. And in that day ye shall ask me nothing. Verily, verily, I say unto you, Whatsoever ye shall ask the Father in my name, he will give it you. – John 16:21-23

44. CHRIST'S GIFTS TO HIS OWN

John 17

ILLUSTRATION:

[44]Once, while walking through a McDonald's restaurant, I saw eight ten-year-old girls celebrating a birthday. The warmth of sheer, unadulterated happiness permeated the gathering.

It was as if a light had been turned on and I could see God's delight. God felt happy that these girls were happy. Their delight, their joy, even their giddiness, gave God great pleasure. Have you ever thought about that—that you can give God great pleasure by enjoying yourself?

If you're a parent, imagine Christmas morning as the young kids tear into presents. Does anything make you happier? Don't moments like these break into the dull routines of life and give us a glimpse of heaven?

The fact that we are children of God—and that Jesus urges us to become like children—speaks of a certain demeanor, a certain delight, a certain trust in God's goodness and favor toward us. While God's servants are not merely his children (he also calls us to sacrificial and mature service), we never become LESS than his children.

1. THE GIFT OF THE LIFE OF GOD

---

[44] GARY THOMAS, "LET'S PLAY," *Men of Integrity* (JANUARY/FEBRUARY 2011)

As thou hast given him power over all flesh, that he should give eternal life to as many as thou hast given him. And this is life eternal, that they might know thee the only true God, and Jesus Christ, whom thou hast sent. – John 17:2-3

2. THE GIFT OF THE NAME OF GOD

I have manifested thy name unto the men which thou gavest me out of the world: thine they were, and thou gavest them me; and they have kept thy word. – John 17:6

3. THE GIFT OF THE WORDS OF GOD

For I have given unto them the words which thou gavest me; and they have received them, and have known surely that I came out from thee, and they have believed that thou didst send me. – John 17:8

Believest thou not that I am in the Father, and the Father in me? the words that I speak unto you I speak not of myself: but the Father that dwelleth in me, he doeth the works. – John 14:10

4. THE GIFT OF SERVICE FOR GOD

I have glorified thee on the earth: I have finished the work which thou gavest me to do. – John 17:4

And all mine are thine, and thine are mine; and I am glorified in them. – John 17:10

According to my earnest expectation and my hope, that in nothing I shall be ashamed, but that with all boldness, as always, so now also Christ shall be magnified in my body, whether it be by life, or by death. – Philippians 1:20

5. THE GIFT OF THE GLORY OF GOD

And the glory which thou gavest me I have given them; that they may be one, even as we are one. – John 17:22

Father, I will that they also, whom thou hast given me, be with me where I am; that they may behold my glory, which thou hast given me: for thou lovedst me before the foundation of the world. – John 17:24

But as many as received him, to them gave he power to become the sons of God, even to them that believe on his name. – John 1:12

6. THE GIFT OF THE LOVE OF GOD

And I have declared unto them thy name, and will declare it: that the love wherewith thou hast loved me may be in them, and I in them. – John 17:26

And hope maketh not ashamed; because the love of God is shed abroad in our hearts by the Holy Ghost which is given unto us. – Romans 5:5

45. CHRIST'S PRAYS FOR HIS OWN

John 17

ILLUSTRATION:

[45]In his book entitled PRAYER, Philip Yancey writes:

As Jesus once prayed for Peter, now he prays for us... In fact, the New Testament's only glimpse of what Jesus is doing right now depicts him at the right hand of God 'interceding for us.' In three years of active ministry, Jesus changed the moral landscape of the planet. For nearly two thousand years since, he has been using another tactic: prayer.

1. THAT THEY BE KEPT BY THE FATHER

I have manifested thy name unto the men which thou gavest me out of the world: thine they were, and thou gavest them me; and they have kept thy word. – John 17:6

And now I am no more in the world, but these are in the world, and I come to thee. Holy Father, keep through thine own name those whom thou hast given me, that they may be one, as we are. – John 17:11

The name of the LORD is a strong tower: the righteous runneth into it, and is safe. – Proverbs 18:10

2. THAT THEY HAVE JOY IN THEMSELVES

---

[45] PHILIP YANCEY, *Prayer* (ZONDERVAN, 2006), P. 88

And now come I to thee; and these things I speak in the world, that they might have my joy fulfilled in themselves. – John 17:13

For the kingdom of God is not meat and drink; but righteousness, and peace, and joy in the Holy Ghost. – Romans 14:17

That which we have seen and heard declare we unto you, that ye also may have fellowship with us: and truly our fellowship is with the Father, and with his Son Jesus Christ. And these things write we unto you, that your joy may be full. – 1 John 1:3-4

3. THAT THEY BE PROTECTED FROM THE DEVIL

I pray not that thou shouldest take them out of the world, but that thou shouldest keep them from the evil. – John 17:15

And lead us not into temptation, but deliver us from evil: For thine is the kingdom, and the power, and the glory, for ever. Amen. – Matthew 6:13

We know that whosoever is born of God sinneth not; but he that is begotten of God keepeth himself, and that wicked one toucheth him not. – 1 John 5:18

4. THAT THEY BE HOLY UNTO GOD

Sanctify them through thy truth: thy word is truth. As thou hast sent me into the world, even so have I also sent them into the world. And for their sakes I sanctify myself, that they also might be sanctified through the truth. – John 17:17-19

Then said Jesus to them again, Peace be unto you: as my Father hath sent me, even so send I you. – John 20:21

5. THAT THEY BE USEFUL UNTO OTHERS

Neither pray I for these alone, but for them also which shall believe on me through their word. – John 17:20

And other sheep I have, which are not of this fold: them also I must bring, and they shall hear my voice; and there shall be one fold, and one shepherd. – John 10:16

6. THAT THEY BE UNITED ONE TO ANOTHER

That they all may be one; as thou, Father, art in me, and I in thee, that they also may be one in us: that the world may believe that thou hast sent me. – John 17:21

There is neither Jew nor Greek, there is neither bond nor free, there is neither male nor female: for ye are all one in Christ Jesus. – Galatians 3:28

For God so loved the world, that he gave his only begotten Son, that whosoever believeth in him should not perish, but have everlasting life. – John 3:16

7. THAT THEY BE GLORIFIED WITH CHRIST

Father, I will that they also, whom thou hast given me, be with me where I am; that they may behold my glory, which thou hast given me: for thou lovedst me before the foundation of the world. – John 17:24

For our light affliction, which is but for a moment, worketh for us a far more exceeding and eternal weight of glory. – 2 Corinthians 4:17

46. THE CHRISTIAN'S RELATIONSHIP TO THE WORLD
John 17

ILLUSTRATION:

[46]"It's not the ship in the water but the water in the ship that sinks it. So it's not the Christian in the world but the world in the Christian that constitutes the danger."

1. THEY ARE TAKEN OUT OF THE WORLD

I have manifested thy name unto the men which thou gavest me out of the world: thine they were, and thou gavest them me; and they have kept thy word. – John 17:6

2. THEY ARE DISTINGUISHED FROM THE WORLD

I pray for them: I pray not for the world, but for them which thou hast given me; for they are thine. – John 17:9

3. THEY ARE IN THE WORLD

And now I am no more in the world, but these are in the world, and I come to thee. Holy Father, keep through thine own name those whom thou hast given me, that they may be one, as we are. – John 17:11

They are not of the world, even as I am not of the world. – John 17:16

---

[46] —Evangelist and pastor J. Wilbur Chapman (1859-1918) MEN OF INTEGRITY MAY/JUNE 2004

4. THEY ARE HATED BY THE WORLD

I have given them thy word; and the world hath hated them, because they are not of the world, even as I am not of the world. – John 17:14

If ye were of the world, the world would love his own: but because ye are not of the world, but I have chosen you out of the world, therefore the world hateth you. – John 15:19

5. THEY ARE KEPT FROM THE GOD OF THIS WORLD

I pray not that thou shouldest take them out of the world, but that thou shouldest keep them from the evil. – John 17:15

6. THEY ARE SENT INTO THE WORLD

As thou hast sent me into the world, even so have I also sent them into the world. – John 17:18

The Spirit of the Lord is upon me, because he hath anointed me to preach the gospel to the poor; he hath sent me to heal the brokenhearted, to preach deliverance to the captives, and recovering of sight to the blind, to set at liberty them that are bruised. – Luke 4:18

Now then we are ambassadors for Christ, as though God did beseech you by us: we pray you in Christ's stead, be ye reconciled to God. – 2 Corinthians 5:20

Then said Jesus to them again, Peace be unto you: as my Father hath sent me, even so send I you. – John 20:21

7. THEY ARE INDWELT FOR THE SALVATION OF THE WORLD

I in them, and thou in me, that they may be made perfect in one; and that the world may know that thou hast sent me, and hast loved them, as thou hast loved me. – John 17:23

I am crucified with Christ: nevertheless I live; yet not I, but Christ liveth in me: and the life which I now live in the flesh I live by the faith of the Son of God, who loved me, and gave himself for me. – Galatians 2:20

47. REVELATIONS IN THE GARDEN

John 18:1-11

ILLUSTRATION:

[47]If you have any knowledge at all of human nature, you know that those who only admire the truth will, when danger appears, become traitors. The admirer is infatuated with the false security of greatness; but if there is any inconvenience or trouble, he pulls back. Admiring the truth, instead of following it, is just as dubious a fire as the fire of erotic love, which at the turn of the hand can be changed into exactly the opposite—to hate, jealousy, and revenge. Christ, however, never asked for admirers, worshipers, or adherents. He consistently spoke of "followers" and "disciples."

Jesus revealed Himself in intimate ways to all who were willing to follow Him as disciples.

1. JESUS' HABIT OF PRAYER

And Judas also, which betrayed him, knew the place: for Jesus ofttimes resorted thither with his disciples. – John 18:2

2. JESUS' KNOWLEDGE OF THE FUTURE

Jesus therefore, knowing all things that should come upon him, went forth, and said unto them, Whom seek ye? – John 18:4

---

[47] —SØREN KIERKEGAARD, DANISH PHILOSOPHER AND THEOLOGIAN (1813–1855)

Then he took unto him the twelve, and said unto them, Behold, we go up to Jerusalem, and all things that are written by the prophets concerning the Son of man shall be accomplished. – Luke 18:31

3. JESUS' CONFESSION CONCERNING HIMSELF

They answered him, Jesus of Nazareth. Jesus saith unto them, <u>I am he</u>. And Judas also, which betrayed him, stood with them. – John 18:5

4. JESUS' POWER OVER HIS ENEMIES

As soon then as he had said unto them, I am he, they went backward, and fell to the ground. – John 18:6

No man taketh it from me, but I lay it down of myself. I have power to lay it down, and I have power to take it again. This commandment have I received of my Father. – John 10:18

5. JESUS' LOVE FOR HIS OWN

Jesus answered, I have told you that I am he: if therefore ye seek me, <u>let these go their way</u>. – John 18:8

6. JESUS' SUBMISSION TO HIS FATHER'S WILL

Then said Jesus unto Peter, Put up thy sword into the sheath: <u>the cup which my Father hath given me, shall I not drink it</u>? – John 18:11

48. CHRIST'S SUFFERINGS AT THE HANDS OF MEN
John 18

ILLUSTRATION:

[48]In his novel Ah, But Your Land Is Beautiful, Alan Paton tells the story of Robert Mansfield, the headmaster of a school in South Africa during the days of apartheid, a cruel system of racial segregation. When Mansfield's school was barred from competing against a black school, he finally took a stand against apartheid and resigned his post. A friend said to him, "You know you will be wounded. Do you know that?"

Mansfield replied, pointing to heaven, "When I go up there ... the Big Judge will say to me, 'Where are your wounds?' If I say I haven't any, he will say, 'Was there nothing to fight for?' I couldn't face that question."

1. BETRAYED BY THE HYPOCRITICAL

They answered him, Jesus of Nazareth. Jesus saith unto them, I am he. And Judas also, which betrayed him, stood with them. – John 18:5

2. DEFENDED BY THE PASSIONATE

Then Simon Peter having a sword drew it, and smote the high priest's servant, and cut off his right ear. The servant's name was Malchus. – John 18:10

---

[48] ALAN PATON, *Ah, But Your Land Is Beautiful* (SCRIBNER, 1996), PP. 66-67

3. SMITTEN BY THE UNREASONABLE

Jesus answered him, If I have spoken evil, bear witness of the evil: but if well, why smitest thou me? – John 18:23

4. DENIED BY THE COWARDLY

And Simon Peter stood and warmed himself. They said therefore unto him, Art not thou also one of his disciples? He denied it, and said, I am not. – John 18:25

5. SHUNNED BY THE SELF-RIGHTEOUS

Then led they Jesus from Caiaphas unto the hall of judgment: and it was early; and they themselves went not into the judgment hall, lest they should be defiled; but that they might eat the passover. – John 18:28

Purge out therefore the old leaven, that ye may be a new lump, as ye are unleavened. For even Christ our passover is sacrificed for us. – 1 Corinthians 5:7

6. QUESTIONED BY THE AMBITIOUS

Then Pilate entered into the judgment hall again, and called Jesus, and said unto him, Art thou the King of the Jews? – John 18:33

Pilate saith unto him, What is truth? And when he had said this, he went out again unto the Jews, and saith unto them, I find in him no fault at all. – John 18:38

And went again into the judgment hall, and saith unto Jesus, Whence art thou? But Jesus gave him no answer. – John 19:9

If any man will do his will, he shall know of the doctrine, whether it be of God, or whether I speak of myself. – John 7:17

7. MOCKED BY THE FRIVILOUS

And the soldiers platted a crown of thorns, and put it on his head, and they put on him a purple robe. – John 19:2

And Herod with his men of war set him at nought, and mocked him, and arrayed him in a gorgeous robe, and sent him again to Pilate. – Luke 23:11

And when I saw him, I fell at his feet as dead. And he laid his right hand upon me, saying unto me, Fear not; I am the first and the last: I am he that liveth, and was dead; and, behold, I am alive for evermore, Amen; and have the keys of hell and of death. – Revelation 1:17-18

49. THE TRIUMPHANT CRY FROM THE CROSS

John 19

ILLUSTRATION:

[49]Author James Herriot, author of *All Creatures Great and Small*, tells of an unforgettable wedding anniversary he and his wife celebrated early in their marriage. His boss had encouraged him to take his wife to a fancy restaurant, but Herriot balked. He was a young veterinarian and couldn't really afford it. "Oh, do it!" the boss insisted. "It's a special day!" Herriot reluctantly agreed and surprised his wife with the news.

En route to the restaurant, Herriot and his wife stopped at a farm to examine a farmer's horse. Having finished the routine exam, he returned to his car and drove to the restaurant, unaware that his checkbook had fallen in the mud. After a wonderful meal, Herriot reached for his checkbook and discovered it was gone. Quite embarrassed, he tried to offer a way of making it up.

"Not to worry," the waiter replied. "Your dinner has been taken care of!" As it was, Herriot's employer had paid for the dinner in advance.

God has done the same for us. Jesus' utterance on the cross, "It is finished," is a Greek term meaning "paid in full."

---

[49] Chuck Tabor, The Time-Gazette, "My bride, Buckeyes, baggage claims...and God," 07/14/2011

When Jesus therefore had received the vinegar, he said, <u>It is finished</u>: and he bowed his head, and gave up the ghost.
– John 19:30

1. JESUS' OWN SUFFERINGS WERE FINISHED

But I have a baptism to be baptized with; and how am I straitened till it be accomplished! – Luke 12:50

2. JESUS' MISSION WAS FINISHED

I have glorified thee on the earth: I have finished the work which thou gavest me to do. – John 17:4

3. THE PROPHECIES CONCERNING JESUS' SUFFERING AND DEATH WERE FINISHED

Searching what, or what manner of time the Spirit of Christ which was in them did signify, when it testified beforehand the sufferings of Christ, and the glory that should follow. Unto whom it was revealed, that not unto themselves, but unto us they did minister the things, which are now reported unto you by them that have preached the gospel unto you with the Holy Ghost sent down from heaven; which things the angels desire to look into. Wherefore gird up the loins of your mind, be sober, and hope to the end for the grace that is to be brought unto you at the revelation of Jesus Christ. – 1 Peter 1:11-13

4. THE WORK OF ATONEMENT WAS FINISHED

Being justified freely by his grace through the redemption that is in Christ Jesus: Whom God hath set forth to be a propitiation through faith in his blood, to declare his righteousness for the remission of sins that are past, through the forbearance of God. – Romans 3:24-25

5. THE MOSAIC LAW WAS FINISHED

Blotting out the handwriting of ordinances that was against us, which was contrary to us, and took it out of the way, nailing it to his cross. – Colossians 2:14

For Christ is the end of the law for righteousness to every one that believeth. – Romans 10:4

Wherefore, my brethren, ye also are become dead to the law by the body of Christ; that ye should be married to another, even to him who is raised from the dead, that we should bring forth fruit unto God. – Romans 7:4

6. THE POWER OF SATAN WAS FINISHED

Forasmuch then as the children are partakers of flesh and blood, he also himself likewise took part of the same; that through death he might destroy him that had the power of death, that is, the devil. – Hebrews 2:14

And having spoiled principalities and powers, he made a shew of them openly, triumphing over them in it. – Colossians 2:15

50. MARY MAGDALENE

John 20:1-18

ILLUSTRATION:

[50]The do-it-yourself, self-help culture of North America has so thoroughly permeated our imaginations that we don't give much sustained attention to the biggest thing of all: resurrection. And the reason we don't give much attention to it is because the Resurrection is not something we can use or manipulate or control or improve on. It is interesting that the world has had very little success in commercializing Easter, turning it into a commodity, the way it has Christmas. If we can't, as we say, "get a handle on it," and use it, we soon lose interest. But resurrection is not available for our use; it is exclusively God's operation.

And certain women, which had been healed of evil spirits and infirmities, Mary called Magdalene, out of whom went seven devils. – Luke 8:2

1. SHE FELT ANXIETY

The first day of the week cometh Mary Magdalene early, when it was yet dark, unto the sepulchre, and seeth the stone taken away from the sepulchre. – John 20:1

2. SHE EXPERIENCED DISAPPOINTMENT

Then she runneth, and cometh to Simon Peter, and to the other disciple, whom Jesus loved, and saith unto them

---

[50] EUGENE H. PETERSON, *Christ Plays in Ten Thousand Places* (EERDMANS, 2005), P. 232

They have taken away the Lord out of the sepulchre, and we know not where they have laid him. – John 20:2

3. SHE DISPLAYED SORROW

But Mary stood without at the sepulchre weeping: and as she wept, she stooped down, and looked into the sepulchre, And seeth two angels in white sitting, the one at the head, and the other at the feet, where the body of Jesus had lain. And they say unto her, Woman, why weepest thou? She saith unto them, Because they have taken away my Lord, and I know not where they have laid him. – John 20:11-13

4. SHE DID NOT SEE JESUS

Jesus saith unto her, Woman, why weepest thou? whom seekest thou? She, supposing him to be the gardener, saith unto him, Sir, if thou have borne him hence, tell me where thou hast laid him, and I will take him away. – John 20:15

5. SHE DISCOVERED THE MASTER

Jesus saith unto her, Mary. She turned herself, and saith unto him, Rabboni; which is to say, Master. – John 20:16

But now thus saith the LORD that created thee, O Jacob, and he that formed thee, O Israel, Fear not: for I have redeemed thee, I have called thee by thy name; thou art mine. – Isaiah 43:1

My soul thirsteth for God, for the living God: when shall I come and appear before God? – Psalm 42:2

6. SHE DEMONSTRATED BOLDNESS

Jesus saith unto her, Touch me not; for I am not yet ascended to my Father: but go to my brethren, and say unto them, I ascend unto my Father, and your Father; and to my God, and your God. – John 20:17

7. SHE SHOWED OBEDIENCE

Jesus saith unto her, Touch me not; for I am not yet ascended to my Father: but go to my brethren, and say unto them, I ascend unto my Father, and your Father; and to my God, and your God. Mary Magdalene came and told the disciples that she had seen the Lord, and that he had spoken these things unto her. – John 20:17-18

And he trembling and astonished said, Lord, what wilt thou have me to do? And the Lord said unto him, Arise, and go into the city, and it shall be told thee what thou must do. – Acts 9:6

51. DOUBTING THOMAS

John 20:24-29

ILLUSTRATION:

[51]After analyzing 600 pages worth of arguments for and against the historicity of Christ's resurrection, Dr. Michael R. Licona concludes that "a good critical scholar must account for the facts with integrity" even when the facts are "in tension with [our] desired outcome." Then he uses the following example from American history:

Long before John Adams became the second U.S. President, in 1770 he was a respected lawyer in New England, where the Boston massacre had just occurred. No lawyers would defend the British soldiers involved for fear of the American public, which had now grown even stronger in its anti-British sentiments. But Adams believed that everyone was entitled to a fair trial. He took the case, the public turned against him, and he lost more than half of his clients.

In a courtroom that was described as crowded and "electrical," Adams argued that the soldiers were innocent .... He then added, "Facts are stubborn things and whatever may be our wishes, our inclinations, or the dictums of our passions, they cannot alter the state of the facts and evidence."

Dr. Licona concludes: "No matter how much one may loathe the idea that Jesus rose from the dead and fantasize about other outcomes, the historical bedrock remains the same .... Jesus' resurrection is the best historical explanation of the relevant historical [evidence]."

---

[51] MICHAEL R. LICONA, *The Resurrection of Jesus* (INTERVARSITY PRESS, 2010), PP. 609-610

1. A LOST OPPORTUNITY

But Thomas, one of the twelve, called Didymus, <u>was not with them when Jesus came</u>. – John 20:24

2. AN EMPHATIC DENIAL

The other disciples therefore said unto him, We have seen the Lord. But he said unto them, Except I shall see in his hands the print of the nails, and put my finger into the print of the nails, and thrust my hand into his side, I will not believe. – John 20:25

3. A HUMBLING REBUKE

Then saith he to Thomas, Reach hither thy finger, and behold my hands; and reach hither thy hand, and thrust it into my side: and be not faithless, but believing. – John 20:27

4. A CONFESSION OF FAITH

And Thomas answered and said unto him, My Lord and my God. Jesus saith unto him, Thomas, because thou hast seen me, thou hast believed: blessed are they that have not seen, and yet have believed. – John 20:28-29

1. Of His AUTHORITY over him. "My *Lord.*"

2. Of His DEITY. "My *God.*"

3. Of his PERSONAL SURRENDER to Him. "*My* Lord and *My* God."

52. HOW JESUS SHOWED HIMSELF

John 21:1-14

ILLUSTRATION:

[52]One sleepy Sunday afternoon when my son was five-years-old, we drove past a cemetery together. Noticing a large pile of dirt beside a newly excavated grave, he pointed and said: "Look, Dad, one got out!" I laughed, but now, every time I pass a graveyard, I'm reminded of the One who got out.

1. THE TIME

1. AFTER A NIGHT OF FAILURE.

Simon Peter saith unto them, I go a fishing. They say unto him, We also go with thee. They went forth, and entered into a ship immediately; and that night they caught nothing. – John 21:3

2. AT THE BREAKING OF THE DAY.

But when the morning was now come, Jesus stood on the shore: but the disciples knew not that it was Jesus. – John 21:4

2. THE MANNER

1. LEADING THEM TO CONFESSION.

---

[52] PHIL CALLAWAY, *Men of Integrity* (MARCH/APRIL 2006)

Then Jesus saith unto them, Children, have ye any meat? They answered him, No. – John 21:5

2. TESTING THEIR FAITH.

And he said unto them, <u>Cast the net on the right side of the ship, and ye shall find</u>. They cast therefore, and now they were not able to draw it for the multitude of fishes. – John 21:6

3. TURNING FAILURE INTO SUCCESS.

And he said unto them, Cast the net on the right side of the ship, and ye shall find. <u>They cast therefore, and now they were not able to draw it for the multitude of fishes</u>. – John 21:6

4. PROVIDING FOR THEIR WANTS.

As soon then as they were come to land, they saw a fire of coals there, and fish laid thereon, and bread. – John 21:9

But my God shall supply all your need according to his riches in glory by Christ Jesus. – Philippians 4:19

5. HAVING FELLOWSHIP WITH THEM.

Jesus saith unto them, Come and dine. And none of the disciples durst ask him, Who art thou? Knowing that it was the Lord. Jesus then cometh, and taketh bread, and giveth them, and fish likewise. – John 21:12-13

And it came to pass, as he sat at meat with them, he took bread, and blessed it, and brake, and gave to them. And their eyes were opened, and they knew him; and he vanished out of their sight. – Luke 24:30-31

Again, he sent forth other servants, saying, Tell them which are bidden, Behold, I have prepared my dinner: my oxen and my fatlings are killed, and all things are ready: come unto the marriage. – Matthew 22:4

(Bonus Sermon)
53. LOVEST THOU ME?

John 21:15

ILLUSTRATION:

[53]Those to whom you minister may not always perfectly understand what you say, but they will soon know whether you love them or not. The secret of many a successful Christian worker is not that he is skilled, knowledgeable, and has endowments which are superior to others, but that those to whom he ministers know that he really cares about them, not in some abstract way, or from sense of duty, but wanting with all his heart the best that God wants for them.

1. LOVE DESIRED

So when they had dined, Jesus saith to Simon Peter, Simon, son of Jonas, lovest thou me more than these? He saith unto him, Yea, Lord; thou knowest that I love thee. He saith unto him, Feed my lambs. He saith to him again the second time, Simon, son of Jonas, lovest thou me? He saith unto him, Yea, Lord; thou knowest that I love thee. He saith unto him, Feed my sheep. He saith unto him the third time, Simon, son of Jonas, lovest thou me? Peter was grieved because he said unto him the third time, Lovest thou me? And he said unto him, Lord, thou knowest all things; thou knowest that I love thee. Jesus saith unto him, Feed my sheep. – John 21:15-17

2. LOVE ACKNOWLEDGED

---

[53] PULPIT HELPS. LEADERSHIP, VOL. 1, NO. 4.

And he turned to the woman, and said unto Simon, Seest thou this woman? I entered into thine house, thou gavest me no water for my feet: but she hath washed my feet with tears, and wiped them with the hairs of her head. Thou gavest me no kiss: but this woman since the time I came in hath not ceased to kiss my feet. My head with oil thou didst not anoint: but this woman hath anointed my feet with ointment. Wherefore I say unto thee, Her sins, which are many, are forgiven; for she loved much: but to whom little is forgiven, the same loveth little. – Luke 7:44-47

3. LOVE MANIFESTED

1. By SEEKING Him.

Jesus saith unto her, Woman, why weepest thou? whom seekest thou? She, supposing him to be the gardener, saith unto him, Sir, if thou have borne him hence, tell me where thou hast laid him, and I will take him away. – John 20:15

2. By CONFESSING Him.

So when they had dined, Jesus saith to Simon Peter, Simon, son of Jonas, lovest thou me more than these? He saith unto him, <u>Yea, Lord; thou knowest that I love thee</u>. He saith unto him, Feed my lambs. – John 21:15

3. By SERVING Him.

So when they had dined, Jesus saith to Simon Peter, Simon, son of Jonas, lovest thou me more than these? He saith unto him, Yea, Lord; thou knowest that I love thee. He saith unto him, <u>Feed my lambs</u>. – John 21:15

With good will doing service, as to the Lord, and not to men. – Ephesians 6:7

4. By SACRIFICING for Him.

And stood at his feet behind him weeping, and began to wash his feet with tears, and did wipe them with the hairs of her head, and kissed his feet, and anointed them with the ointment. – Luke 7:38

Then Paul answered, What mean ye to weep and to break mine heart? for I am ready not to be bound only, but also to die at Jerusalem for the name of the Lord Jesus. – Acts 21:13

Thank You for Your Investment in this Book!

Barry L. Davis, D.Min.

If we can help you with more ministry resources please feel free to visit us at:

www.pastorshelper.com

Made in the USA
Middletown, DE
10 March 2020

86139891R00104